SISTERHOOD
A QUILTING TRADITION

11 HEARTWARMING PROJECTS TO PIECE & APPLIQUÉ

Nancy Lee Murty

C&T PUBLISHING

Text copyright © 2011 by Nancy Lee Murty

Artwork copyright © 2011 by Nancy Lee Murty and C&T Publishing, Inc.

Publisher: Amy Marson

Creative Director: Gailen Runge

Acquisitions Editor: Susanne Woods

Editor: Liz Aneloski

Technical Editors: Carolyn Aune and Gailen Runge

Cover/Book Designer: Kristen Yenche

Production Coordinator: Zinnia Heinzmann

Production Editor: Alice Mace Nakanishi

Illustrators: Nancy Lee Murty and Kirstie Pettersen

Photography by Christina Carty-Francis and Diane Pedersen of C&T Publishing, Inc., unless otherwise noted

Published by C&T Publishing, Inc., P.O. Box 1456, Lafayette, CA 94549

Library of Congress Cataloging-in-Publication Data

Murty, Nancy Lee, 1970-

Sisterhood-a quilting tradition : 11 heartwarming projects to piece & appliqué / Nancy Lee Murty.

p. cm.

ISBN 978-1-60705-192-3 (softcover)

1. Quilting--Patterns. 2. Appliqué--Patterns. I. Title.

TT835.M92 2011

746.46'041--dc22

2010033968

Printed in China

10 9 8 7 6 5 4 3 2 1

DEDICATION
To my quilting sisters everywhere

ACKNOWLEDGMENTS

A special thank-you to my parents, John and Linda Davis, for encouraging me to follow my dreams. A big hug and thank-you to Peggy Davis for all the encouragement and unending support. Heartfelt thanks to Jean Welch and Meghan Welch for their willingness to jump in with enthusiasm and make the projects their own. Special thanks to Marty Wilson and Terri Wilson for always making fabric shopping fun.

A sincere thank-you to Joanne Galasso, Margaret Landon, and Nana's Quilt Shop, as well as to MaryKay Kaczmarek, Lynn Artieri, and Donald Bunn, for your outstanding machine quilting skills and readiness to tackle the big boys!

I would like to thank the wonderful team at C&T for helping to make this a truly wonderful and joyous experience.

And to my husband, Paul Murty—I owe you 1,000 thank-yous for the endless support and countless offers to fix dinner. You are a true gift!

CONTENTS

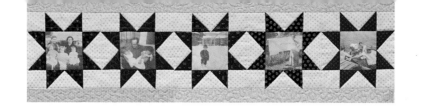

INTRODUCTION

Sewing has always been a part of my family's heritage. As a child, I remember my sister, Peggy, and me sitting on the floor in my grandmother's sewing room with a tin of buttons between us. There we sat, stringing buttons with needle and thread, discussing which colors we liked best or exclaiming something like, "Oh, Grandma, look at the flower on this one." We entertained ourselves with those buttons for hours. Next visit, the buttons would be back in the tin, ready to string all over again. Those are such happy memories and the beginning of many hours spent with family and friends in the sewing room.

The quilting sisterhood has grown in our family, with my mother's sister, Jean Welch, and her daughter, Meghan, having been bitten by the quilt bug. Over the years, I've had the great fortune of meeting many wonderful people through quilting, and many cherished friends have been folded into this sisterhood as well.

Throughout this book, I've tried to share some of the things I've discovered in my quilting journey. I also want to encourage you to find your own creative voice. Please feel free to alter any of the projects to fit your desires, to change the colors and fabrics to reflect your personal style, and to share quilting with those you love.

Above left: *My great-grandmother, Esther Brown; my sister, Peggy; and me.*   Above center: *My mother, Linda Davis.*
Above right: *My cousin, Meghan Welch.*   Bottom left: *My sister, Peggy; my grandmother, Martha Davis; and me.*
Bottom right: *My aunt, Jean Welch, and her daughter, Meghan Welch.*

GETTING STARTED

Over the 25 plus years I've been a quilter, my sewing spaces have ranged from the kitchen table of my first apartment to my own dedicated sewing studio in our current home. But the most unique sewing area belonged to my sister, who converted the large walk-in closet of her apartment into a little sewing room.

Whether you have a dedicated space in your home or you sew on the kitchen table, good lighting, a comfortable chair, and a design board can make it a more pleasurable experience. After a day spent sewing in the studio, Toni Foster, a good friend, couldn't believe that her back didn't bother her and realized it was the chair that had made the difference. I prefer a chair that has a height adjustment, good back support, and no arms, so it's easier to get up and walk over to the cutting table.

As I get older, I am realizing how important good lighting is at both the sewing machine and the cutting table. Position the light someplace in front of you, so you are not working in your own shadow.

Before I had a design wall, I used to lay out the quilt blocks on the floor. Inevitably, after all the blocks were sewn together, I would discover a block upside down or turned. Being able to put the quilt blocks on the design wall helps prevent this from happening. There is also just something about being able to step back from the work and evaluate it while looking at it straight on.

Maybe you can't incorporate a full design wall into your sewing space. Not to worry—a smaller design board can easily be made to slip behind the couch or under a bed for storage.

To create a small, lightweight design board, purchase a sheet of foamcore at a local office supply or craft store and flannel or felt fabric at least 10″ larger than the sheet of foamcore. Center the foamcore on the flannel or felt fabric. Fold the flannel or felt fabric around the edge of the foamcore and tape it to the back with 2″-wide masking tape.

If you need a larger design board, sheets of foam insulation board can be purchased at the local hardware store. Cover the insulation board with flannel or felt fabric in the same manner as for the small design board.

One addition to my sewing area that really made a difference and I would be lost without is the sewing table my dad made. It allows my sewing machine to be recessed, so the machine's sewing area is flush with the table surface. This has made a huge difference in the ease of handling a quilt and the quality of my machine quilting.

Regardless of where you spend your time quilting, there are a few essential tools to keep handy, as well as several additional items to help make quilting all that much more fun. You will need the following items for the projects in this book.

ROTARY CUTTER AND SELF-HEALING CUTTING MAT

A rotary cutter with a sharp blade and an 18″ × 24″ or larger cutting mat are essential tools in quiltmaking.

ROTARY RULERS

The three rulers I use the most in my quiltmaking are an 8½″ × 24″ acrylic ruler for cutting strips and borders, an 8½″ bias square ruler for trimming half-square triangle units to size, and a 20½″ square ruler, which is great for cutting appliqué blocks to size.

IRON AND IRONING BOARD

I like to use an iron that produces a good amount of steam and has a nice point.

MARKING PENCIL

I prefer to use a mechanical pencil for marking sewing lines because of the fine, crisp line. I like the Sewline Fabric Pencil (by Westek Incorporated) because the lead is made to wash out of fabric and it comes in several different colors, including white.

THREAD

I use cotton sewing thread for piecing and a variety of cotton and polyester threads for machine quilting.

PINS AND NEEDLES

I like thin silk pins and prefer long straw or sharp needles for hand stitching. A variety of different size sewing machine needles are good to keep on hand, but 70/10 are good for general sewing.

SCISSORS

I keep a small pair of appliqué scissors and a small pair of snips with a curved blade by the sewing machine to clip threads while sewing. A large pair of scissors is nice for cutting fusible adhesive and freezer paper. Although raised with designated "paper" and "fabric" scissors, I must confess that all the scissors in my studio are multifunctional.

SEAM RIPPER

Oh, if only we didn't need a reverse sewing apparatus, but we all make mistakes that need to be corrected.

QUICK QUARTER II

I use this tool (by Quilter's Rule) all the time to mark the diagonal sewing lines when making half-square triangle units and flying geese units.

100% COTTON FABRIC

I only work with high-quality 100% cotton fabric. One of the questions I hear most is, "Do you prewash your fabric?" The answer is, "It depends." Because I like appliqué, I generally try to wash new fabrics before using them in a project or adding to my fabric "collection." However, there are exceptions when I don't prewash. For example, if I am making a quilt that uses a printed panel or border design and the pattern calls for specific cut sizes, I will not prewash the fabric, as washing may change the size of the printed design.

One last thing I recommend before jumping in and getting started is to grab a cup of tea, sit in a comfy chair, and read through the following chapters—who knows, maybe you'll pick up a new technique, tip, or idea. Also, briefly look over the construction steps for the project you will be starting to get an idea of where you will be going as you progress through the construction.

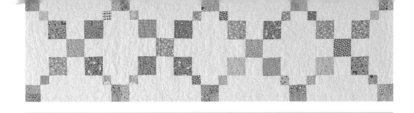

MAKING CHOICES

Selecting fabric for a project seems to be a step you either love or hate in quilting—I happen to love it.

In fabric selection, it's all about relationships—the relationship of each fabric with the fabrics around it in the quilt. As you make your selections, lay out the fabrics on the table or place them on the floor. Arrange fabrics that will be next to each other in the project so they are next to each other on the table. This way you can see how well the fabrics play with each other. If a fabric stands out or draws too much attention, remove it from the pile.

I ask myself a few questions while selecting fabrics for a project: Do the prints of the fabrics vary in scale and texture? Do the fabrics have a range in value—light, medium, and dark? Overall, are the fabrics primarily warm or cool in color? The answers to these questions assist me in deciding which fabrics to add to or eliminate from a project. The biggest thing to remember is there are no wrong decisions—follow your intuition. It's all about what you like as you make the selections.

To add spark to a quilt, invite a stranger to the party! I often add a fabric that is different from all the others. For example, if I have selected mostly warm colors, I will add a blue, or if the fabrics are mostly blue and green, I may add a red or pink.

After you have selected the fabrics for a project, I recommend that you cut a small square of each fabric and glue or tape all of the squares to an index card. Next to each fabric square write where the fabric is to be used in the project (for example, star points) and the assembly letters. You will then have this card to reference as you work on the quilt project. I like to use the card as a bookmark to keep my place while working on the project.

Intimate Connections

Pale Yellow (A, B)
Yellow/Gold (C, D)
Rose (E)
Blue Floral (F)
Rose Paisley (G)
Pink florals (5) (H, I)

Dinner for Two

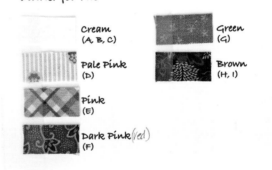

Cream (A, B, C)
Pale Pink (D)
Pink (E)
Dark Pink (red) (F)
Green (G)
Brown (H, I)

Perennial Ties

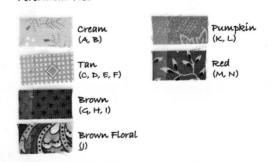

Cream (A, B)
Tan (C, D, E, F)
Brown (G, H, I)
Brown Floral (J)
Pumpkin (K, L)
Red (M, N)

PATCHWORK BASICS

YARDAGE REQUIREMENTS

All yardages given are for 42"-wide fabric, with 40" of usable fabric width after prewashing and removing selvages. For the best use of the yardage, cut fabric in the order given in the cutting directions.

USING THE ROTARY CUTTER

Many quilters like to use the grid printed on the cutting mat, but I like to ignore this grid. I only use the ruler to straighten and measure when cutting my fabric. Fold the fabric in half, bringing the selvages together, and position the fabric on the cutting mat with the fold toward you. Align the bottom of the ruler with the fold of the fabric and make a vertical cut to create a straight fabric edge. Begin cutting strips, measuring from the cut edge. Every once in a while, trim the edge to reestablish a straight edge.

Cut the largest size strips first. That way, if you make a mistake, a smaller strip can still be cut from it.

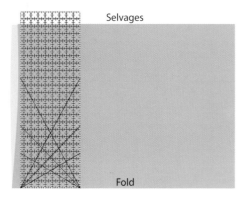

Selvages

Fold

For some projects, you will need to cross cut squares along one or both diagonals to create triangles. Place the cut fabric squares on the cutting mat and position the ruler diagonally across the square so the edge of the ruler sits in the corners of the fabric square. Cut along the edge of the ruler. If the project calls for cutting along both diagonals, rotate the cutting mat 90°, without disturbing the fabric on the mat, and reposition the ruler diagonally. Line up the edge of the ruler with the other two opposite corners and cut.

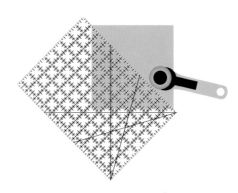

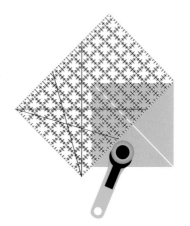

MACHINE PIECING

Always remember to join fabrics with right sides together. The one secret to successful machine piecing is sewing with an accurate ¼" seam allowance. Most sewing machine companies sell a ¼" presser foot made specifically for quilting, which is especially helpful. You can also make a seam guideline with a strip of masking tape.

ASSEMBLY-LINE SEWING

Assembly-line sewing (or chain sewing) can make piecing a quilt quicker and reduces the number of long threads that will need to be clipped. Continue to feed units through the sewing machine, one after another, without snipping the threads in between each unit. When you are finished sewing, clip the threads between each unit and press as instructed.

My sister and I keep a stack of cut 2" × 3½" rectangles by the sewing machine and feed these through at the end of each segment of assembly-line sewing. Before we know it, we have a little stack of blocks waiting for something fun to be done with them at a later date.

TIP

Wind several bobbins when you start a new project; it'll save you time later.

PRESSING TECHNIQUES

One key to piecing that is often overlooked is good pressing. I like to press with plenty of steam. I also work from the front side of the block, when possible, so I don't have to fight to keep all the seam allowances lying flat.

I like to work toward myself. Lay the sewn units on the ironing board, with the fabric you are pressing the seam allowance toward (usually the darker fabric) facing up. Run the iron over the seam first. Then flip the top fabric down and press. Position the iron so the edge is parallel to the seam.

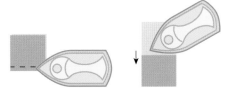

CONSTRUCTION TECHNIQUES

HALF-SQUARE TRIANGLE UNITS

Several projects in this book use half-square triangle units in their construction. The units will be trimmed down to their final dimensions to create a uniform size, making final piecing of the quilt block easier.

1. Position the Quick Quarter tool (see page 6) diagonally across the wrong side of the lighter fabric. Using a mechanical pencil, draw a line on each side of the Quick Quarter tool, as well as in the slotted openings along the center of the tool.

If you don't have a Quick Quarter tool, position a ruler diagonally across the lighter square. Place the edge of the ruler in both corners and then draw a dashed line to mark the center diagonal. Position the ruler's ¼" mark along the center dashed line and draw a solid line. Repeat for the other side of the center dashed line.

2. With right sides together, pair the marked lighter square with a dark fabric square. Sew along the 2 outside drawn lines. Cut along the center dashed line. Press the seam allowances toward the darker fabric.

3. Using a square ruler and rotary cutter, trim each half-square triangle unit to the size specified in the project instructions. Start by lining up the ruler's 45° diagonal line with the seam and centering the desired finished size within the fabric square. Trim off the right and top edges of the fabric square.

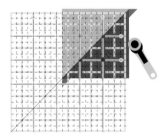

4. Turn the fabric square 180° and realign the ruler, matching the diagonal line with the seam and the 2 cut edges with the desired finished size marks on the ruler. Trim the 2 remaining (right and top) sides of the fabric square.

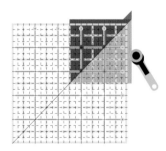

5. Repeat Steps 1–4 to yield the number of half-square triangle units required for the project.

FLYING GEESE UNITS

I just love this method for making flying geese. I've included a few tips to help you achieve more accurate flying geese units. For this technique, gather 4 small squares and 1 large square, as instructed in the project directions.

1. Position the Quick Quarter tool diagonally across the wrong side of the smaller squares, lining up the corners of the square with the bar's center line. Using a mechanical pencil, lightly draw a line next to each side of the Quick Quarter bar, as well as in the slotted openings along the center of the tool. Mark the remaining 3 small squares.

If you don't have a Quick Quarter tool, position a ruler diagonally across the smaller squares. Place the edge of the ruler in both corners and then draw a dashed line to mark the center diagonal. Position the ruler's ¼" mark along the center dashed line and draw a solid line. Repeat for the other side of the center dashed line.

2. With right sides together, pair up the large square with 2 marked small squares, setting the 2 small squares at opposite corners of the large square. Sew along the 2 outside drawn lines. Separate by cutting along the center dashed line. Press the seams toward the small triangles.

3. With right sides together, place a small marked square on each unit from Step 2. Sew along the outside drawn lines. Cut along the dashed lines to separate. Press the seams toward the small triangle. Trim away the "dog-ears" (the little points that extend beyond the rectangular shape of the goose unit). Trim even with the goose rectangle. You should now have 4 flying geese units.

THE "A" WORD— APPLIQUÉ

Appliqué isn't for everyone. If you think of appliqué as the "A" word, here are a few suggestions for alternatives to use instead: Paint the appliqué design onto the fabric using textile paint, such as Stewart Gill or Liquitex. Substitute a large-scale print for the appliqué blocks in a project. Or, use the appliqué pattern as a quilting or embroidery design. If you like the quilt's design, don't let the fact that it features appliqué stop you.

In addition to the standard quilting supplies, the following tools are helpful for appliqué:

- Spray starch

- Clover Bias Tape Maker, ¼" (6mm)

- Small scissors with a fine, sharp point

- Open-toe presser foot

- Roxanne Glue Baste-It

- Lightbox—may be helpful, but is not necessary

MAKING BIAS STEMS

Some appliqué incorporates a bias stem or vine in the design. Stems are usually the first thing positioned in appliqué. The ends should extend under the flowers by ½". I usually cut ½ yard of fabric into bias strips for stems, so that I have stems ready for the next several appliqué projects.

1. With an acrylic ruler and rotary cutter, straighten both side edges of the fabric (page 8). Open the fabric to a single thickness and place it on the cutting mat. Line up the ruler's 45° mark with the fabric's straightened edge. Cut along the ruler. Rotate the cutting mat, measuring from the diagonal edge of the fabric. Cut strips ⅝" wide for ¼" stems and 1⅛" wide for ½" stems.

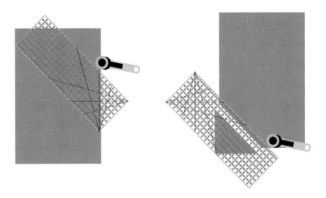

2. If necessary, sew the cut bias strips together to reach the required length for the stems in the project. Press the seam allowances open. Trim the seam allowance even with the strip's outside edge.

3. Place the bias strip wrong side up on the ironing board. Spray the bias strip with spray starch. Press. Feed the end of the bias strip into the Bias Tape Maker and pull the strip through, ironing as you go.

FUSIBLE APPLIQUÉ METHOD

It's hard to beat the speed and ease of using fusible webbing for appliqué projects. For a quilt with a soft feel, be sure to select a lightweight fusible webbing product, such as Lite Steam-A-Seam.

1. The patterns in this book have already been reversed to make it easier for you. Begin by tracing each piece of the appliqué design onto the paper side of the fusible webbing. As you trace the design, add ¼" in the overlap areas. Be sure to trace each piece individually and to transfer the pattern letter. Roughly cut out each appliqué shape, leaving about ¼" of fusible webbing around the outside edge.

2. Following the manufacturer's directions for the fusible product you are using, iron the fusible web appliqué shapes to the wrong side of the selected fabrics. Cut out each appliqué piece on the traced line.

3. When positioning the appliqués, fold the background square in half and lightly press. Repeat folding in the opposite direction to mark the center. Fold the background square in half diagonally and lightly press to mark. Repeat for the opposite diagonal.

4. Remove the paper backing from each appliqué piece and arrange the appliqués on the background fabric, referring to the quilt photo as necessary. When you are happy with the placement, iron to fuse the appliqué in place according to the manufacturer's directions.

5. Finish off the raw edges of the appliqué with a machine-sewn blanket stitch or another decorative stitch. You can either match the thread color to the appliqués or choose contrasting colors. I like to use several different contrasting colors of thread for some added fun in the finished quilt.

INVISIBLE MACHINE APPLIQUÉ

I just love this method for appliqué and use it frequently in my quilts. The real beauty of this process is in the final result—a quilt that looks like it was hand appliquéd but with the speed of the sewing machine. If you like, use the appliqué design (below) to work along with the directions as you become familiar with this method.

In addition to the supplies previously mentioned, you will also need:

- Water-soluble gluestick—I like Westek's Sewline Fabric Glue Pen because of its smaller tip and available refills.

- Tailor's awl or stiletto—such as Alex Anderson's 4-in-1 Essential Sewing Tool (by C&T Publishing)

- Invisible thread in both clear and smoke colors—I like YLI.

- Freezer paper—I find Reynolds brand works the best.

PREPARING THE PAPER TEMPLATES

The patterns in this book have already been reversed to make it easier for you. Trace each appliqué shape onto the paper side of the freezer paper. Draw arrows to indicate an area where the seam allowance will not need to be turned under, because it will be overlapped by another appliqué shape. Cut along the drawn line.

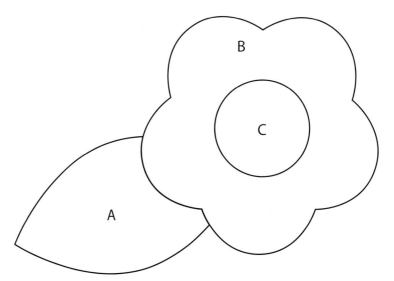

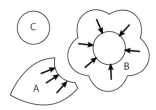

Many of the projects feature multiple appliqués. A time-saving trick is to divide the number of appliqués to be traced by 4. For example, if you need to trace 36 leaves, divide 36 by 4 to equal 9. Trace 9 leaves on the freezer paper and layer the traced freezer paper with 3 additional sheets of the same size. Staple through the center of each traced leaf to hold the 4 layers of freezer paper together. Cut out each leaf. Remove the staples and transfer the original pattern letter to each cut leaf.

IRONING TEMPLATES TO FABRIC

1. With the shiny side of the freezer paper against the wrong side of the selected fabric, iron the freezer paper template in place using a dry iron (no steam). If multiple freezer paper templates are being ironed to the fabric, leave at least ½″ between the templates.

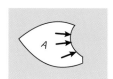

2. Using sharp scissors, cut out the templates, using a ¼″ seam allowance around each shape. To make it easier to pin the appliqué units together in a later step, leave more fabric on the side with the arrows. The extra fabric will be trimmed away later.

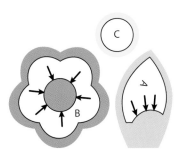

GLUING THE SEAM ALLOWANCES

I find it easiest to work in a counterclockwise direction (left-handed quilters should work in a clockwise direction) and to apply the water-soluble glue to 2″–3″ of the ¼″ seam allowance at a time. Gently fold the glued seam allowance over and press to the freezer paper. If you are too forceful in folding over the seam allowance, you might fold the freezer paper over as well, causing the appliqué shape to become distorted. Remember not to glue the seam allowance where the arrows are drawn.

Smooth Curves

Place the appliqué flat on a table. With the point of an awl or stiletto, gently pull the seam allowance over the edge of the freezer paper in a downward motion so the fabric goes around the curve. Tighter curves require smaller bites of fabric to be pulled around the edge of the freezer paper. I like to use a tailor's awl, but the point of a seam ripper or small pair of scissors will also work. Continue working around the curve, applying glue as needed.

From time to time, turn over the appliqué to evaluate how it looks from the front. Make any adjustments necessary for a smooth outside edge. If you have a bump or sharp point along the curved edge, it is most likely caused by a tuck in the seam allowance. Flip the appliqué back over and loosen the seam allowance where the bump is. Reapply glue if necessary and distribute the seam allowance, creating a couple of small wrinkles instead of the original tuck.

Outside Points

Fold and press the right seam allowance to the freezer paper. The fabric's folded edge should extend beyond the point of the freezer paper. Apply glue to the left seam allowance and gently fold over and press to the freezer paper.

Inside Points, or V's

If an appliqué has an inside point, I like to start there. With the tip of small, sharp scissors, make one clip down the center of the V, stopping a few threads short of the freezer paper's edge. Apply glue to the seam allowance on both sides of the V. Gently fold back the seam allowance and press to the freezer paper, pushing your thumb toward the center of the appliqué to catch any loose threads.

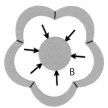 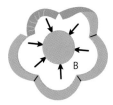

TIP

If the weather is warm, try storing the water-soluble glue pen in the refrigerator to keep it from getting too soft.

GETTING THE SEWING MACHINE READY

1. Wind a bobbin with a neutral-colored cotton thread.

2. Thread the machine with invisible thread on top. Match the color of the invisible thread to the appliqué, using clear thread for light fabrics and smoke-colored thread for medium and dark fabrics. Use an open-toe presser foot so you can easily see the appliqué's edge while stitching.

3. Set the machine for a narrow zigzag stitch. I find a stitch width of around 1mm and a length of about 1.5mm works well for me. I also have to loosen the top tension a little (between 1 and 2). If the top tension is too tight, it will pull the bobbin thread through so it shows on top. Stitch several inches on 2 layers of scrap fabric to check the tension and the stitch width and length. Make any necessary adjustments.

CREATING APPLIQUÉ UNITS

Instead of handling the entire background to sew all the appliqués in place, units of appliqué can be prepared ahead of time. To me, this is one of the biggest benefits of this method; whenever possible, I like to create appliqué units.

1. Position 2 overlapping appliqués and pin to secure.

2. Place the appliqué under the presser foot so the needle pierces the appliqué's edge. Take 2 or 3 stitches in place by reducing the stitch length to 0; this will anchor the threads on the back.

3. Begin stitching around the top appliqué's outside edge so the majority of the zigzag stitch is in the top appliqué. You should be stitching over the folded fabric edge.

4. At the end of the sewing, take another 2 or 3 stitches in place to lock the threads by reducing the stitch length. When sewing around curves, stop stitching with the needle down, raise the presser foot, pivot the appliqué, lower the presser foot, and then continue sewing.

5. On the wrong side of the appliqué, use a small pair of scissors to trim away the back layer of fabric, leaving a ¼″ seam allowance. Be careful not to cut through the freezer paper and appliqué below.

6. Place the appliqué unit (in this example, the flower) with the next appliqué shape (the leaf) and pin together. Remember that the design will be a mirror image of the drawing. Most of the designs in this book are symmetrical, so this won't happen; however, the tree for *Family and Friends* (page 34) will be a mirror image. Stitch as before, trimming away the extra fabric to leave a ¼″ seam allowance.

SEWING THE APPLIQUÉ TO THE BACKGROUND

1. To help position the appliqués, fold the background square in half and lightly press to mark the center. Repeat folding in the opposite direction. Then fold the background square in half diagonally and lightly press to mark. Repeat for the opposite diagonal.

2. If necessary, position the bias stems on the background square first. Instead of pins, use Roxanne Glue Baste-It to hold the stems in place. Then place all the appliqué units and individual appliqués in place on the background fabric. Pin the appliqués in place.

3. Sew around each appliqué, as well as along both sides of the stems. Be sure to lock your stitching at the beginning and end. Once all the appliqués have been sewn to the

background fabric, flip over the appliqué block, so that the wrong side of the background fabric is facing up. Pinch the background fabric and use a small pair of scissors to make a small clip where each appliqué shape is. Do not cut the freezer paper. Trim away the background fabric from behind each appliqué shape, leaving a ¼″ seam allowance. You should see the freezer paper from each appliqué shape. *Do not* cut the background fabric behind the bias stems; only trim where there is freezer paper to be removed.

REMOVING THE PAPER

1. To dissolve the glue, place the sewn appliqué block in lukewarm water for 5 to 10 minutes.

2. Working from the back, remove all the freezer paper. If you are struggling to remove the freezer paper, check to be sure that the glue has dissolved.

TIP

To easily remove the freezer paper from behind appliqué that has been added to the finished quilt top, use a spray bottle to wet the back of the appliqué. Once the glue has dissolved, remove the paper.

3. Rinse to remove any remaining glue residue.

4. Squeeze excess water from the appliqué block and lay it flat on a clean towel. Roll up the towel. Place the rolled towel on the floor and step on it—go ahead, jump up and down if you want.

5. Unroll the towel and hang the appliqué block on the towel bar to dry.

6. Place the dry appliquéd block wrong side up on an ironing board. Press the appliqué, making sure the seam allowances lie flat.

7. Trim the appliqué block to its final size, if instructed to do so in the project directions.

PUTTING IT ALL TOGETHER

Before sewing the pieced and/or appliquéd blocks together to create the quilt center, lay them out on the design wall or floor. Assess the quilt's overall appearance and balance. Make any necessary adjustments to the block placement before sewing the quilt together.

When working on a large quilt, sew the assembled rows together in pairs and then sew the pairs together, creating 2 halves. Then sew the halves of the quilt together. This keeps you working in smaller sections, which are easier to handle.

ADDING BORDERS

DIAGONAL SEAMS

I usually use diagonal seams to join fabric strips because doing so distributes bulk in the binding and helps camouflage the seam in the borders.

1. Square up the ends of the cut fabric strips, removing the selvages.

2. With right sides together, place the 2 strips at right angles. Because of the way the strips lie on top of each other, the corner of the bottom strip won't be visible. Lightly draw a little dot to mark the top strip where the corner of the bottom strip is. Using a small ruler as a straight edge, draw a diagonal line from the corner of the top strip to the little dot (the corner of the bottom strip).

3. Sew on the drawn line. Trim to a ¼″ seam allowance. Press the seam open.

PINNING THE BORDER STRIPS TO THE QUILT CENTER

The measurements given for the cut border lengths are mathematically correct, but you may need to make adjustments based on your personal sewing style. Pieced borders may need extra attention for sewing accurately, as a small difference in seam width multiplied by numerous seams can result in a pieced border being too long or too short.

1. When sewing borders to the quilt center, fold the border strip in half to find the center. Then finger-press or insert a pin to mark the center. Fold again so the marked center lines up with the ends of the rectangle; find the quarters and mark. Repeat this process for the side of the quilt center, marking the center and quarters.

2. With right sides together, line up the center and quarter marks on the border strip with the center and quarter marks on the side of the quilt; pin together. Sew and press as directed in the project directions.

FINISHING UP

Growing up with a mother who quilted, I never really thought about the "quilt as desired" statement that is so prevalent in quilt instructions. That was, not until my Aunt Jean started quilting, when I saw that statement from a beginner's point of view. If you need additional quilting guidance, please look at the quilt photos for ideas and inspiration.

PIECING THE QUILT BACKING

When preparing a quilt backing, the rule of thumb is to make it 8″ larger than the quilt top. If you are sending your quilt to a longarm quilter, check to see what size backing he or she prefers. Unless a project is small or you are using an extra-wide quilt back, you will have to piece the backing fabric. In general, quilts 72″ wide or smaller will be pieced with one seam running vertically. For large quilts, the back is pieced with two horizontal seams.

For quilts up to 72″ wide

For quilts larger than 72″ wide

TIP

If you are not the most confident machine quilter, choosing a backing fabric with a busy print will help hide the quilting.

LAYERING AND BASTING THE QUILT SANDWICH

Taking the time to properly layer and baste a quilt is one of the most important steps in determining how straight the final quilt will be. Because I machine quilt, I use safety pins to baste the layers together. For this method, I find working on a carpeted floor works best.

1. Place the quilt backing, wrong side up, on a carpeted floor.

2. Smooth out any wrinkles and secure the edges with straight pins—push the pins straight through the fabric into the carpet and padding.

3. Lay the batting on top of the backing and smooth out any wrinkles.

4. With the right side up, center the quilt top over the batting and backing. Smooth out any wrinkles.

5. Using a 12′ tape measure, measure both diagonals (from corner to corner) across the quilt. Gently adjust the quilt top until both measurements are the same. Now the quilt is "squared up." I learned this trick from my woodworker father.

6. Use rustproof safety pins to pin every 4″, starting in the center and working out toward the edges. Do not close the pins yet.

7. Pull out the straight pins used to secure the backing fabric.

8. Pick the layered quilt off the floor and lay it flat on the ironing board or dining room table.

9. Close all the safety pins.

Marking and Quilting

I'm usually starting to think about how I am going to quilt the project during the pin-basting process. If you plan to outline an appliqué design (also known as quilting in the ditch), you may not need to mark the quilt. For custom quilting, I've become quite fond of marking my quilt using stencils and a swipe pad filled with Miracle Chalk. The Miracle Chalk disappears with the heat of an iron. I also find it easier to mark a few blocks at a time rather than marking the entire quilt at once. Lines or crosshatching can be quilted using various widths of painter's tape as a guide or the guide bar included with some purchased walking feet.

1. Begin quilting in the center, working your way out toward the edge.

2. Trim the extra batting and backing to 1" beyond the edge of the quilt top before machine quilting the border. This prevents accidentally catching the extra backing fabric in the quilting.

3. I like to press my quilts after I have finished machine quilting them, both to achieve that nice pressed finish and to remove the Miracle Chalk markings.

4. Using a large ruler and rotary cutter, trim off the extra batting and backing fabric so they are even with the quilt top.

Binding

For most quilts, I like to have a ½" finished binding width; however, for a few projects, narrower ¼" binding is preferred.

1. Cut the number of strips specified for the project and join them into one continuous length using diagonal seams (page 16).

2. Fold over the corner at 45°, wrong sides together, and press.

3. Fold the strip in half lengthwise and press along the entire length of the binding.

ATTACHING THE BINDING

1. With the front of the quilt right side up, place the folded end of the binding in the middle of one side of the quilt. Line up the raw edges of the binding with the quilt's outside edge. Start sewing about 10" from the folded end of the binding, using a ½" seam allowance (use a ¼" seam allowance for the narrower ¼"-wide binding). Stop sewing ½" (¼") from the corner of the quilt, pivot, and sew a diagonal seam out to the corner of the quilt.

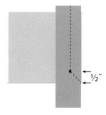

2. Rotate the quilt to sew down the next side. Fold up the binding strip and finger-press the binding along the sewn diagonal.

3. Fold the binding strip back down, lining up the raw edge with the quilt's edge. The top fold should be even with the quilt's top edge, creating a square corner.

4. Sew from the top edge down the side of the quilt, stopping ½" (¼") from the bottom corner. Sew a diagonal seam out to the quilt corner as in Step 1. Continue for the quilt's remaining corners. Stop sewing about 20" from the starting point.

JOINING THE ENDS

1. Lay the quilt with the binding strip ends to be joined facing up. Place the binding end with the pressed fold flat over the quilt, lining up the raw edges of the binding with the quilt top.

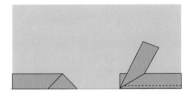

2. Lay the other end of the binding strip so it overlaps the first binding strip end, lining up the raw edges with the quilt's edge.

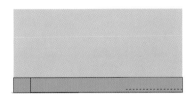

3. Open the top binding strip, so the wrong side is facing up. Pin the edge of the binding strip to the folded-over triangle from the strip underneath—indicated with a dotted line in the illustration. Pin only to the folded-over corner of the lower binding strip.

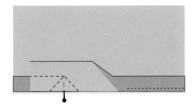

4. Open the bottom binding strip, so both the top and bottom are open and the right sides are together. The strips should be at right angles to each other. You will need to maneuver or fold the quilt to achieve this step. Pin together. Sew a diagonal seam. If you flip the quilt over so the quilt top and binding are facing the table, you will be able to sew in the pressed diagonal crease.

5. Remove the pins and lay the quilt flat to check the fit. If everything checks out, cut off the extra binding fabric, leaving a ¼" seam allowance. Press the seam open and then press the binding strip back in half along the length. Sew the binding to the side of the quilt with a ½" (¼") seam allowance.

6. With the quilt face up on the ironing board, press the binding over toward the outside edge. Fold the binding around to the back of the quilt and sew down by hand.

LABELING YOUR QUILT

Someone once told me a quilt is not done until its label is sewn on. I'm not always the best at getting labels on the backs of my quilts, but I have a few suggestions to help. To stabilize the fabric, iron a square of freezer paper to the wrong side of the label. Use a textile marker to write the information on the fabric label and then hand stitch it to the back of the quilt.

I also recommend keeping a journal or some kind of visual record of your projects. It's fun to look back at all the quilts you have made.

INTIMATE CONNECTIONS

Made by Nancy and Paul Murty and machine quilted by Joanne Galasso

▪ Intimate Connections ▪

Finished blocks: 12″ × 12″

Finished quilt: 72″ × 72″

Skill level: Intermediate

One of the first things my sister, Peg, did after moving to her new home out of state was visit her local shop and join the quilt guild. It was a simple way to connect to her new community and meet great people with whom she had plenty in common. Quilting groups, whether a small circle or a large guild, are typically generous, caring groups offering support—not only to other quilters and their families, but also to their communities. Who wouldn't want to be associated with that sisterhood!

I designed *Intimate Connections* with these strong and growing bonds in mind. Think of the individual stars as quilters, families, or the community. The flowing leaf appliqué surrounding each star joins them together, creating a growing, flowering connection that unites us all.

MATERIALS

Light yellow: 2⅜ yards for background

Yellow: 1⅛ yards for background

Rose: ¾ yard for star points

Blue floral: ½ yard for star centers

Paisley: ½ yard for star centers

Green: ½ yard each of 4 fabrics for leaves

Gray green: ⅓ yard for stems

Dark red: fat quarter or ¼ yard each of 2 fabrics for flower petals

Red: ⅛ yard for flower centers

Blue: ⅛ yard for small circles

Pink prints: ⅝ yard each of 5 fabrics for borders

Binding: ¾ yard

Backing: 4½ yards

Batting: 80″ × 80″

CUTTING

The letter following each cut size corresponds to the letters in the block assembly diagrams.

Light yellow

- Cut 5 strips 12½″ × width of fabric; subcut into:

  13 squares 12½″ × 12½″ (A)

  6 squares 4¼″ × 4¼″ (B)

- Cut 2 strips 4¼″ × width of fabric; subcut into:

  18 squares 4¼″ × 4¼″ (B)

Yellow

- Cut 3 strips 7¼″ × width of fabric; subcut into:

  12 squares 7¼″ × 7¼″ (C)

  6 squares 4¼″ × 4¼″ (D)

- Cut 2 strips 4¼″ × width of fabric; subcut into:

  18 squares 4¼″ × 4¼″ (D)

Rose

- Cut 5 strips 3⅞″ × width of fabric; subcut into:

  48 squares 3⅞″ × 3⅞″ (E)

Blue floral

- Cut 3 strips 3⅞″ × width of fabric; subcut into:

  24 squares 3⅞″ × 3⅞″; cut in half diagonally (F)

Paisley

- Cut 2 strips 4¾″ × width of fabric; subcut into:

  12 squares 4¾″ × 4¾″ (G)

Pink prints

From each of 5 fabrics:

- Cut 2 strips from each fabric 6½″ × width of fabric; subcut into:

  4 rectangles 12½″ × 6½″ (H) to make 20 total

  1 square 6½″ × 6½″ (I) to make 5 total (one will not be used)

Binding

- Cut 8 strips 3″ × width of fabric.

Star Blocks

Follow the arrows for pressing direction.

HALF-SQUARE TRIANGLE CORNER UNITS

1. With the 24 B pieces and the 24 D pieces, make 48 half-square triangle units (pages 9 and 10) and press.

2. Trim the units to 3½" × 3½".

FLYING GEESE UNITS

Working with 12 C pieces and 48 E pieces, construct 48 flying geese units (page 10). The finished flying geese units should measure 3½" × 6½".

CENTER SQUARE-IN-A-SQUARE UNITS

1. Fold all the sides of G in half and finger-press to mark the center. Gently fold the long side of F in half and finger-press to mark the center. Try not to stretch or pull the fabric as you fold and mark the triangles—this is the bias edge, and it will stretch.

2. With right sides together and matching center creases, sew an F to 2 opposite sides of G and press. Sew an F to the 2 remaining sides of G and press.

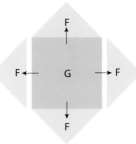

3. Repeat for the remaining units. The center square-in-a-square units should measure 6½" × 6½".

ASSEMBLING THE UNITS

1. Following the diagram for placement, lay out 4 flying geese, 1 center square-in-a-square, and 4 half-square triangles.

2. Working across in 3 rows, sew the units together and press.

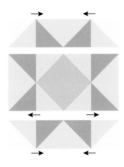

3. Sew the 3 rows together and press.

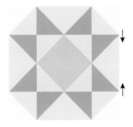

4. Repeat the process to make 12 Star blocks. The blocks should measure 12½"× 12½", including the ¼" seam allowance.

APPLIQUÉ BLOCKS

Prepare the appliqués, using the appliqué method of your choice (pages 11–15).

1. Prepare 52 bias stems, each ¼" × 7½" (page 11). Using the method of your choice, trace and prepare the appliqués (page 25).

2. Position the appliqués on background A in this order: 4 stems first, followed by 16 leaves, and then a center flower. Make sure the leaves are placed within ½" of the fabric square's outside edge. Sew the appliqués to the background fabric.

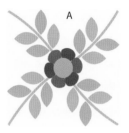

3. Repeat Step 2 for a total of 13 appliqué blocks.

You will have leaf and small circle appliqués left over; they will be stitched to the quilt top during assembly.

QUILT ASSEMBLY AND APPLIQUÉ

Refer to the quilt photo (page 20) and the quilt assembly diagram (page 24); follow the arrows in the diagrams for pressing direction.

Because appliqué needs to be added to the joined star and appliqué blocks, as well as to the outer border, sew the quilt together in sections rather than in the traditional row method.

1. To make the top row of the quilt, start in the corner and sew an H to the top of an appliqué block; press.

2. Sew an I to an H and press.

3. Sew an I/H unit to the side of the appliqué block unit and press.

4. Add the appliqué leaves that are indicated in the quilt assembly diagram with a black outline.

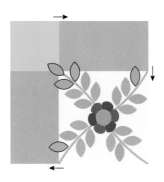

5. Sew an H to the top of a Star block and press.

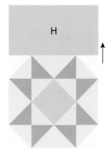

6. Sew a star unit to the corner appliqué unit. Press the seam toward the appliqué unit.

7. Add the appliqué leaves that are indicated in the quilt assembly diagram with a black outline.

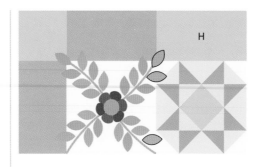

8. Continue working across the quilt to complete the row, adding another I/H unit to the end of the quilt's top row. Always press the seams toward the appliqué block.

9. To make the second row, sew together 3 Star blocks, alternating with 2 appliqué blocks and adding the appliqué as you go. Sew an H piece to each end of the row. Press the seams toward the appliqué block.

10. Sew rows 1 and 2 together and press. Add the appliqué leaves and small circles.

11. Continue sewing each row and sewing on the appliqué pieces. The bottom row is made the same as the top row of the quilt (Steps 1–8).

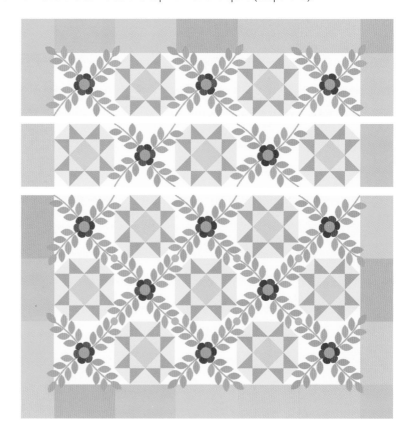

FINISHING UP

Refer to Finishing Up (pages 17–19) for details on completing your quilt.

1. Piece the backing fabric with one vertical seam.

2. Layer the quilt top, batting, and backing fabric and baste.

3. Quilt as desired.

4. Bind using a ½" seam allowance.

5. Don't forget your quilt label.

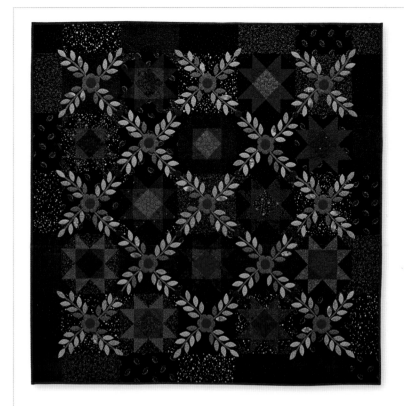

Made by Peggy Davis

Peggy chose to use dark fabrics in her quilt for a dramatic effect.

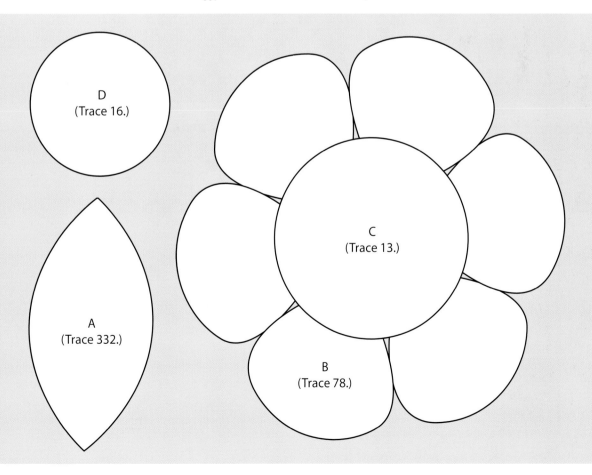

D
(Trace 16.)

C
(Trace 13.)

A
(Trace 332.)

B
(Trace 78.)

HERITAGE

Made by Nancy Murty and machine quilted by Joanne Galasso

Heritage

Finished block: 6″ × 6″

Finished quilt: 92½″ × 100″

Skill level: Experienced Beginner

Quilting is part of our heritage, passed down through the generations. I believe we all have a sisterhood connection with our grandmothers and great-grandmothers that should be cherished. We sometimes lose track of the fact that these women were not always as we remember them. They were women with growing families who faced many of the same issues and challenges we do, often without the resources and support that we enjoy today.

While choosing fabrics and sewing this project, I would often think of my grandmother and wonder what her thoughts had been when she was sewing. What wonderful or challenging things were happening in her life? In my own way, I was spending special time with her, continuing and strengthening the bond that started so long ago.

MATERIALS

Medium to dark: 16 fat quarters for blocks and binding

Dark pink: ⅜ yard for sashing

Light: 9⅛ yards for background, sashing, and outer border

Backing: 8⅝ yards

Batting: 100″ × 108″

Quick Quarter II tool (*optional*)

CUTTING

The letter following each cut size corresponds to the letters in the block assembly diagrams.

Medium to dark
From each of 14 fabrics:

- Cut 3 strips 3¼″ × 21″; subcut into:

  16 squares 3¼″ × 3¼″ (A) to make 224 total

- Cut 1 strip 2½″ × 21″; subcut into:

  8 squares 2½″ × 2½″ (B) to make 112 total

- Cut 1 strip 3″ × 21″ for binding.

From 1 fabric:

- Cut 1 strip 3¼″ × 21″; subcut into:

  4 squares 3¼″ × 3¼″ (A)

  2 squares 2½″ × 2½″ (B)

- Cut 4 strips 3″ × 21″ for binding.

From 1 fabric:

- Cut 4 strips 3″ × 21″ for binding.

Dark pink
- Cut 5 strips 2″ × width of fabric; subcut into:

  90 squares 2″ × 2″ (C)

Light
- Cut 7 strips 6½″ × width of fabric; subcut into:

  42 squares 6½″ × 6½″ (D)

- Cut 12 strips 6½″ × width of fabric; subcut into:

  223 rectangles 2″ × 6½″ (E)

- Cut 19 strips 3¼″ × width of fabric; subcut into:

  228 squares 3¼″ × 3¼″ (F)

- Cut 29 strips 2½″ × width of fabric; subcut into:

  456 squares 2½″ × 2½″ (G)

- Cut 15 strips 2″ × width of fabric; subcut 10 strips into:

  20 rectangles 14″ × 2″ (H)

  Reserve 5 strips for sashing (I).

- Cut 11 strips 2½″ × width of fabric for outer border.

Shoo Fly Blocks

Follow the arrows for pressing direction.

1. With 228 A's and 228 F's, make half-square triangle units (pages 9 and 10) and press.

2. Trim each unit to 2½" × 2½".

3. Sort the half-square triangle units by fabric into 15 stacks.

4. From the same fabric, lay out 1 B and 4 G's with 4 A/F half-square triangle units to form the Shoo Fly block.

TIP

Lay out the units for the pieced block on a square quilter's ruler for easy transport to the sewing machine.

---

5. Sew the units together, working across the block in 3 rows; press. Sew the rows together and press.

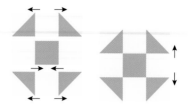

6. Repeat Steps 4 and 5 to make 114 Shoo Fly blocks. Each block should measure 6½" × 6½", including the ¼" seam allowance.

TIP

For good sewing machine maintenance, clean the bobbin area of lint every time you put in a new bobbin.

Quilt Assembly

Refer to the quilt photo (page 26) and the quilt assembly diagram (next page).

1. For I, join the 5 reserved 2" strips, using diagonal seams (page 16). From this long sewn strip, cut 2 pieces 89" long.

2. Lay out all the components, following the assembly diagram for placement. Sew together the components in each row, pressing seam allowances toward the sashing (E and H).

3. Sew the rows together and press the seams toward the light sashing rectangles (E, H, and I).

4. Using diagonal seams (page 16), join the 11 light 2½" outer border strips into one long strip. Cut 2 strips 2½" × 96½" for the sides and 2 strips 2½" × 93" for the top and bottom.

5. Sew the 96½" strips to the sides of the quilt and press the seams toward the border. Sew a 93" strip to the top and bottom of the quilt and press the seams toward the border.

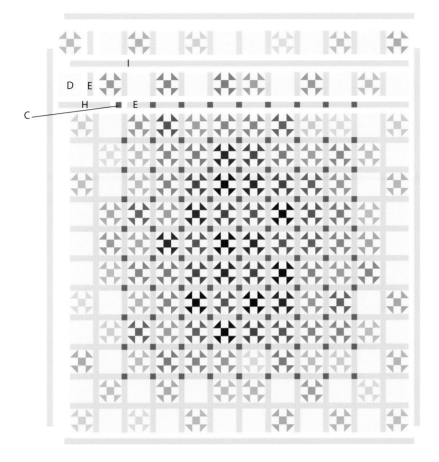

FINISHING UP

Refer to Finishing Up (pages 17–19) for details on completing your quilt.

FINISHING UP

1. Piece the backing fabric with 2 horizontal seams.

2. Layer the quilt top, batting, and backing fabric and baste.

3. Quilt as desired.

4. Bind using a ½" seam allowance.

5. Don't forget your quilt label.

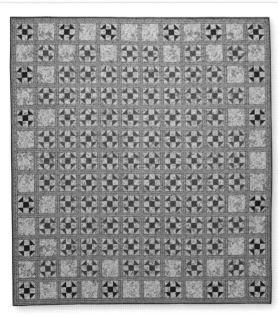

Made by Marty and Terri Wilson

Marty and Terri used soft floral fabric with a contrasting stripe fabric for the sashing to create a romantic feel.

Made by Peggy Davis

Peggy chose a dark print for the background in her pieced blocks and a second fabric for the sashing.

GENERATIONS

Made by Peggy Davis

▪ Generations ▪

Finished block: 8″ × 8″

Finished quilt: 62½″ × 74″

Skill level: Intermediate

Through the years, my family has tended to cherish special places and favorite memories over extravagant heirlooms. On one of my father's early visits to see my mother, he brought an acorn from a favorite spot near his family's farm. He planted the acorn, and it grew to be a strong and beautiful oak tree.

Years later, when my mother's parents had passed and the family farm was being sold, my father again gathered acorns. This time they were planted at my parent's house. Eventually, sprouted acorns from this tree were given to my mother's siblings, so they could all have a piece of home, wherever they lived. The tradition continues today, as I have a smaller, but no less special, oak tree growing in my yard—part of that same lineage.

It is easy to connect the story of our oak to the growth of our families, continuing on through generations. This quilt is to honor that strength and remind us of our unmistakable connection to the past, as well as the promise of the future.

MATERIALS

Pale green: 2½ yards for appliquéd blocks and setting triangles

Light green: 2 yards for pieced blocks and border

Green: 1¼ yards for pieced blocks

Assorted red/purple prints: 1 yard total for leaves

Assorted blue prints: ½ yard total for moon appliqués

Assorted green prints: ⅓ yard total for center-diamond appliqués

Binding: ⅞ yard

Backing: 4⅝ yards

Batting: 70″ × 82″

CUTTING

The letter following each cut size corresponds to the letters in the block assembly diagrams.

Pale green
- Cut 2 strips 12⅝″ × width of fabric; subcut into:

  5 squares 12⅝″ × 12⅝″, cut in half diagonally in both directions (A)

  2 squares 6⅝″ × 6⅝″, cut in half diagonally (B)

- Cut 5 strips 10″ × width of fabric; subcut into:

  20 squares 10″ × 10″ (C)

Light green
- Cut 8 strips 4½″ × width of fabric; subcut into:

  120 rectangles 2½″ × 4½″ (D)

- Cut 8 strips 3½″ × width of fabric for border.

Green
- Cut 4 strips 4½″ × width of fabric; subcut into:

  30 squares 4½″ × 4½″ (E)

- Cut 8 strips 2½″ × width of fabric; subcut into:

  120 squares 2½″ × 2½″ (F)

Binding
- Cut 8 strips 3″ × width of fabric.

PIECED BLOCK

Follow the arrows for pressing direction.

1. Lay out 4 D pieces with the 4 F pieces and 1 E.

2. Working across the block in 3 rows, sew the fabric pieces together and press. Sew the rows together and press.

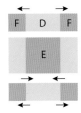

3. Repeat Steps 1 and 2 to make 30 pieced blocks. The blocks should measure 8½″ × 8½″, including the ¼″ seam allowance.

APPLIQUÉ BLOCKS

Prepare the appliqués, using the appliqué method of your choice (pages 11–15).

1. Using the method of your choice, trace and prepare the appliqués (page 33).

2. Follow the quilt photo for placing the appliqués on C. After all the appliqués have been sewn to the background square and the paper removed, trim the block to 8½″ × 8½″, centering the appliqué. Repeat this step for a total of 20 appliqué blocks.

QUILT ASSEMBLY

Refer to the quilt photo (page 30) and the quilt assembly diagram (below).

1. Lay out the quilt, alternating the pieced blocks with the appliqué blocks and placing an A at the end of each diagonal row. Place a B in each corner.

2. Sew the blocks together in diagonal rows. Press the seam allowances toward the appliqué blocks. Sew the rows together and press the seams to one side.

BORDER

1. Join the eight 3½″ border strips with diagonal seams (page 16) to create one long continuous strip. Cut 2 strips 3½″ × 68⅜″ for the sides and 2 strips 3½″ × 63″ for the top and bottom borders.

2. Sew the 68⅜″ strips to the sides of the quilt and press the seams toward the border. Sew a 63″ strip to the top and bottom of the quilt and press the seams toward the border.

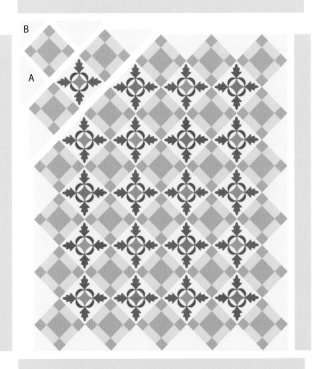

FINISHING UP

Refer to Finishing Up (pages 17–19) for details on completing your quilt.

1. Piece the backing fabric with one vertical seam.

2. Layer the quilt top, batting, and backing fabric and baste.

3. Quilt as desired.

4. Bind using a ½″ seam allowance.

5. Don't forget your quilt label.

Made by Meghan Welch and machine quilted by Jean Welch

Meghan, who is not a fan of appliqué, used a large floral print in place of the appliqué blocks.

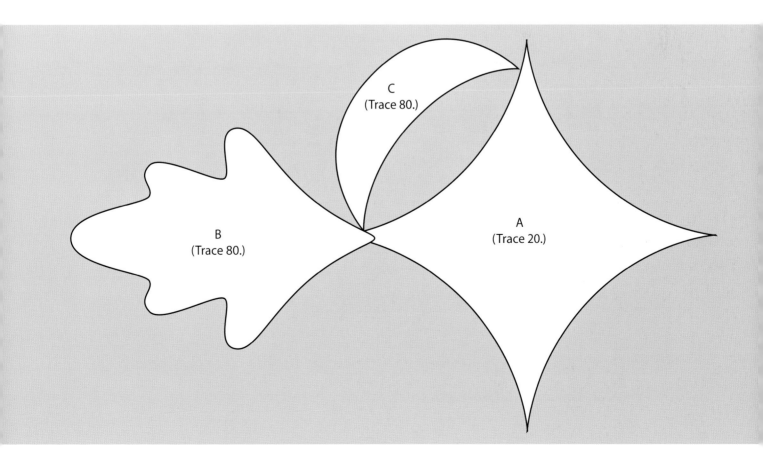

FAMILY AND FRIENDS

Made by Nancy Murty and machine quilted by Joanne Galasso

▪ Family and Friends ▪

Finished blocks: 18″ × 18″ and 6″ × 6

Finished quilt: 60″ × 60″

Skill level: Experienced Beginner

Over the years, quilts have often given insight into the lives of the quilter who crafted the piece. We all have admired the exquisite Baltimore Album, which recounts with beautiful detail the highlights of a family's life. I am equally moved by the simple patchwork quilt, in which pieces of Grandma's favorite dress or the drapery fabric from Great-grandma's house hide. How wonderful to pass along such cherished memories to future generations.

Family and Friends offers a design that will truly be cherished for years and generations to come. The quilt includes several opportunities for personal touches, such as names, pictures, or favorite fabrics. I chose to place old family photos in the centers of my Star blocks.

MATERIALS

Assorted dark fabrics: 1¼ yards total for stars, leaf, and berry appliqués, *or* ¾ yard assorted dark fabrics and 7 inkjet fabric sheets if you are using photos for the star center (I like Printed Treasures Inkjet Fabric Sheets by Milliken.)

Lightest: 1⅛ yards for Star block background

Light #1: ⅝ yard for appliqué background

Light #2: ⅝ yard for appliqué background

Brown: 1 fat quarter for tree appliqués

Border and binding: 1⅞ yards

Backing: 3⅞ yards

Batting: 68″ × 68″

CUTTING

The letter following each cut size corresponds to the letters in the block assembly diagrams.

Assorted dark fabrics
- Cut 28 squares 3½″ × 3½″ (A).
- Cut 224 squares 2″ × 2″ (B).

Lightest
- Cut 5 strips 3½″ × width of fabric; subcut into:

  100 rectangles 3½″ × 2″ (D)
- Cut 7 strips 2″ × width of fabric; subcut into:

  112 squares 2″ × 2″ (E)

  12 rectangles 3½″ × 2″ (D)

Light #1 and #2
From each fabric:

- Cut 1 square 20″ × 20″; cut in half diagonally (C).
- Cut 1 square 18½″ × 18½″ (C).

Border and binding
- Cut 4 strips 6½″ × *length of fabric*; subcut into:

  2 strips 6½″ × 48½″ for border

  2 strips 6½″ × 60½″ for border
- Cut 4 strips 3″ × *length of fabric* for binding.

Appliqué Blocks

Prepare the appliqués (pattern pullout page P1), using the appliqué method of your choice.

BACKGROUND BLOCKS

To make 2 of the background blocks, sew a C triangle of light #1 to a C triangle from light #2. Press the seam toward the darker fabric. Trim to 18½" × 18½". Make 2.

CREATING A TREE

1. Using the method of your choice, trace and prepare the appliqués on the pullout pattern sheet.

2. Position the appliqués on C in this order: the tree branches and trunk first, followed by the leaves, and finishing with the round berries. The 2 leaves at the end of branch B will be added after the 4 appliqué blocks are sewn together. Sew the appliqués to the background square. Repeat for a total of 4 appliqué blocks, each measuring 18½" × 18½". Position the appliqué on the half-square triangle background blocks as shown in the quilt photo (page 34).

FINISHING THE QUILT CENTER

1. Refer to the quilt photo (page 34) and sew the 4 appliqué blocks together in 2 horizontal rows of 2 blocks each. Press the seams in opposite directions.

2. Sew the 2 rows together and press the seam to one side. The pieced center should measure 36½" × 36½".

3. Position and stitch the last 8 leaves over the seams to complete the quilt center.

ADDING THE WORDS

There are several ways to add the text. I chose to outline the text using a brown Pigma marker (textile marker). My sister used a water-soluble marking pen to outline the text and then used a heavyweight thread to outline the text as she machine quilted the project. My mother chose to embroider the words.

Whichever method you choose, place the appliquéd blocks over the pattern (pullout page P1) and lightly trace the text onto the background fabric. If the fabric is dark and you can't see the text through it, use a lightbox or window.

Stem Stitch

If you choose to embroider the words, you can use a stem stitch and backstitch.

1. With 2 strands of knotted embroidery floss, bring the needle up through the fabric at A. Insert the needle at B and come out again at C.

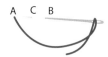

2. Insert the needle at D and come out at B. Continue in the same manner, always inserting the needle ahead of and coming out at the previous stitch.

Backstitch

1. Knot 2 strands of embroidery floss and come up through the fabric at A. Insert the needle at B and come up at C.

2. Insert the needle again at B and come out at D. Continue in the same manner, always inserting the needle into the end of the last stitch.

STAR BLOCKS

Follow the arrows in each diagram for pressing direction.

1. Draw a diagonal line on the wrong side of all the B's.

<table>
<tr><td>TIP</td></tr>
</table>

The Sewline Fabric Pencil (by Westek Incorporated) with white or pink lead is great for marking darker fabrics.

2. With right sides together, position a marked B next to one end of a D. Sew on the drawn line and press. Trim away the 2 extra layers of fabric, leaving a ¼" seam allowance. Repeat, sewing a second B to the opposite end of D. Repeat to make 112 flying geese units.

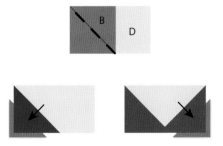

3. Lay out 4 B/D flying geese, 1 A, and 4 E's to create a star.

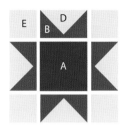

4. Sew the Star block together, working across in 3 rows; press. Sew the 3 rows together and press the seams toward the center. Repeat to create 14 Star blocks. Blocks should measure 6½" × 6½", including the ¼" seam allowance.

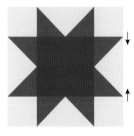

5. With the remaining flying geese units and pieces A and E, construct an additional 14 Star blocks. *Note:* Press the seams *away* from the centers when sewing the rows together in this set of 14 blocks.

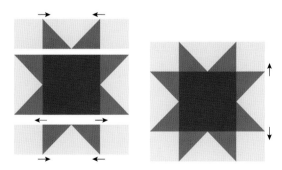

BORDERS

Refer to the quilt photo (page 34) and the quilt assembly diagram (at right).

1. Position the 28 Star blocks around the appliqué center. Alternate the Star blocks created in Steps 3 and 4 (page 37) with seams pressed toward the center and those created in Step 5 (page 37) with seams pressed away from the center (indicated by red and blue stars in the assembly diagram).

2. Sew together 2 sets of 6 Star blocks to create the side border strips. Press the seam allowances in one direction. Sew a border strip to the right and left sides of the appliqué center. Press the seams away from the center.

3. Sew together 2 sets of 8 Star blocks to create the top and bottom border strips. Press the seam allowances in one direction. Sew a border strip to the top and bottom of the appliqué center. Press the seams toward the border.

4. Add the 6½″ × 48½″ strips to the sides of the quilt and press the seams toward the outside edge. Sew the 6½″ × 60½″ strips to the top and bottom of the quilt. Press the seam allowances toward the outer border.

FINISHING UP

Refer to Finishing Up (pages 17–19) for details on completing your quilt.

1. Piece the backing fabric with one vertical seam.

2. Layer the quilt top, batting, and backing fabric and baste.

3. Quilt as desired.

4. Bind using a ½″ seam allowance.

5. Don't forget your quilt label.

Made by Peggy Davis

For her version, Peggy used a limited number of fabrics and colors.

Made by Linda Davis and machine quilted by Margaret Landon

Linda used a dark background for her quilt.

Made by Meghan Welch and machine quilted by Nancy Murty

Meghan, not being a fan of appliqué, used Stewart Gill paint to create the center appliqué design.

CROSS MY HEART

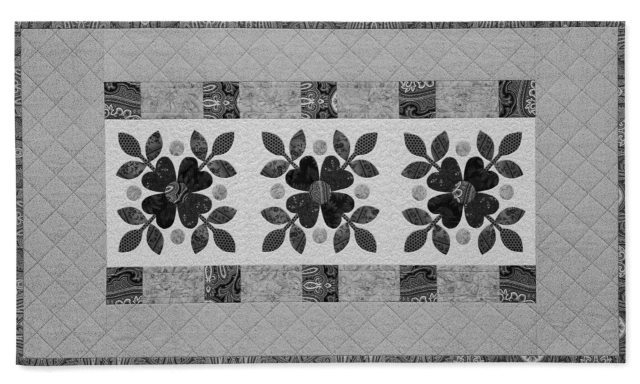

Made by Nancy Murty

When we were young girls, we would "cross our hearts" and swear to keep the secrets that were entrusted to us. Now that we're all a little bit older, we may not cross our hearts, but we still understand the importance of having those special people we can confide in, as well as being there for those close to us. The trust that we have in each other is one of the strongest bonds of our "sisterhood" and the foundation for lasting friendships.

Finished blocks: 12" × 12"

Finished table runner: 50" × 27"

Skill level: Experienced Beginner

MATERIALS

Light tan: ½ yard for block background

Red paisley: ¼ yard for checkerboard strip and flower center appliqués

Gold: ⅓ yard for checkerboard strip and circle appliqués

Tan: 1 yard for border

Red: 9" × 14" piece for heart appliqués

Dark red: 9" × 14" piece for darker heart appliqués

Yellow green: ¼ yard for leaves and stem

Green: ¼ yard for leaves

Binding: ½ yard

Backing: 1⅔ yards

Batting: 58" × 35"

CUTTING

The letter following each cut size corresponds to the letters in the block assembly diagrams.

Light tan

■ Cut 3 squares 13½" × 13½" (A).

Red paisley

■ Cut 1 strip 3½" × width of fabric; subcut into:

  2 squares 3½" × 3½" (B)

Gold

■ Cut 1 strip 5¾" × width of fabric.

Tan

■ Cut 2 strips 7½" × width of fabric; subcut into:

  2 rectangles 7½" × 27½" (C)

■ Cut 2 strips 5" × width of fabric; subcut into:

  2 rectangles 5" × 36½" (D)

Binding

■ Cut 5 strips 3" × width of fabric.

APPLIQUÉ BLOCKS

Prepare the appliqués, using the appliqué method of your choice (pages 11–15).

1. Prepare 12 bias stems, each ¼" × 3" (page 11). Using the method of your choice, trace and prepare the appliqués (page 43).

2. Position the appliqués on background A in this order: stems first, followed by the heart petals and leaves, then the flower center and smaller circles. Sew the appliqués to the background fabric. Trim the block to 12½" × 12½", centering the appliqué.

3. Repeat Step 2 for a total of 3 appliqué blocks.

4. Sew the appliqué blocks together, pressing the seam allowances in one direction. The sewn appliqué blocks should measure 12½" × 36½".

BORDERS

Follow the arrows in each diagram for pressing direction.

CHECKERBOARD STRIP

1. With right sides together, sew the remainder of the 3½″ red paisley strip to the 5¾″ gold strip. Press. Cut the strip set into 3½″ segments for a total of 8 segments.

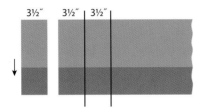

2. Sew together 2 sets of 4 segments. Sew a B to the end of each segment and press. Each checkerboard strip should measure 3½″ × 36½″, including the ¼″ seam allowance.

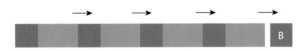

3. Sew a checkerboard strip to both long sides of the appliquéd center and press.

OUTER BORDER

1. Sew a D to each long side of the table runner and press.

2. Sew a C to each end of the table runner and press.

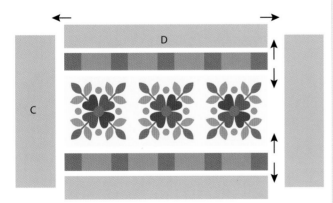

FINISHING UP

Refer to Finishing Up (pages 17–19) for details on completing your table runner.

1. Layer the table runner, batting, and backing fabric and baste.

2. Quilt as desired.

3. Bind using a ½″ seam allowance.

4. Don't forget your quilt label.

Made by Jean Welch

Jean used pink, red, and green with a dark border to finish her project.

Made by Terri Wilson and machine quilted by Marty Wilson

A monochromatic palette in shades of blue gives a soothing effect to this table runner.

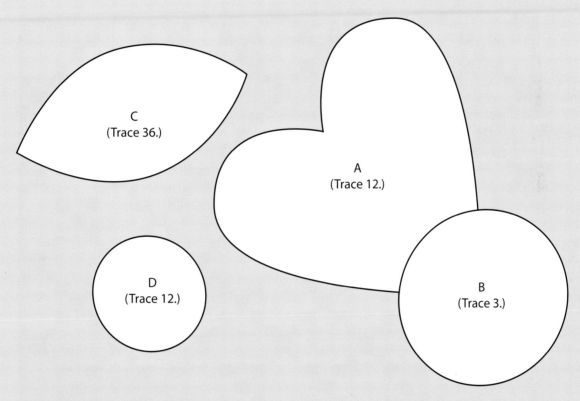

C
(Trace 36.)

A
(Trace 12.)

B
(Trace 3.)

D
(Trace 12.)

Appliqué for *Cross Your Heart*

CHAINS OF FRIENDSHIP

Made by Nancy Murty and machine quilted by Joanne Galasso

Finished blocks: 7½″ × 7½″, 7½″ × 6″, and 6″ × 6″

Finished quilt: 87″ × 97½″

Skill level: Experienced Beginner

There is a certain strength associated with the links of a chain. Each link is supported by its connection to the other links. And just like in a good friendship, each link is counted on to support the others when needed. The sisterhood is alive and well in the bonds of friendship we create through our quilting, and our quilting sisters are often the first to pitch in when we need them. I've created this design to honor these bonds.

The connection between the bonds of friendship and the chains of this quilt design is easy to see. As the links and bonds intertwine, the individual pieces grow into a beautiful singular design.

MATERIALS

Light: 31 fat quarters

Dark: 14 fat quarters

Binding: ¾ yard

Backing: 8¼ yards

Batting: 95″ × 105″

CUTTING

The letter following each cut size corresponds to the letters in the block assembly diagrams.

Light
From each of 21 of the fat quarters:

■ Cut 1 strip 8″ × 21″; subcut into:

5 rectangles 3½″ × 8″ (A) to make 105 total

■ Cut 1 strip 3″ × 21″; subcut into:

6 squares 3″ × 3″ (B) to make 126 total

■ Cut 2 strips 2″ × 21″; subcut into:

20 squares 2″ × 2″ (C) to make 420 total

From each of 6 of the fat quarters:

■ Cut 4 strips 3½″ × 21″; subcut into:

8 rectangles 3½″ × 8″ (A) to make 48 total

1 square 3″ × 3″ (B) to make 6 total

■ Cut 1 strip 3″ × 21″; subcut into:

6 squares 3″ × 3″ (B) to make 36 total

From each of 4 of the fat quarters:

■ Cut 2 strips 8″ × 21″; subcut into:

9 rectangles 3½″ × 8″ (A) to make 36 total (You will not use 1.)

Dark
From each of the fat quarters:

■ Cut 3 strips 3″ × 21″; subcut into:

15 squares 3″ × 3″ (D) to make 210 total

■ Cut 3 strips 2″ × 21″; subcut into:

30 squares 2″ × 2″ (E) to make 420 total

Binding
■ Cut 10 strips 2″ × width of fabric.

Pieced Blocks

Follow the arrows in each diagram for pressing direction.

RAIL BLOCKS

1. Sew 2 assorted A's together along the 8″ side to form a Rail block; press.

2. Repeat Step 1 to make 91 Rail blocks that measure 6½″ × 8″, including the ¼″ seam allowance. Use 6 of the left-over pieces for the final quilt assembly.

TIP

Set the A pieces beside the sewing machine. As you piece the other blocks for the quilt, feed the paired rectangles through the machine as you finish each sewing step. Before you know it, the stack of rectangles will be gone, and you'll have finished this step for the quilt.

NINE-PATCH BLOCKS

1. Lay out 4 assorted B's with 5 assorted D's to form a Nine-Patch block.

2. Sew the 3″ squares together, working across the block in 3 rows; press. Sew the rows together and press.

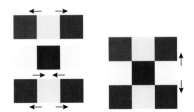

3. Repeat Steps 1 and 2 to make 42 Nine-Patch blocks. The blocks should measure 8″ × 8″, including the ¼″ seam allowance.

SIXTEEN-PATCH BLOCKS

1. Lay out 8 assorted C's with 8 assorted E's to form a Sixteen-Patch block.

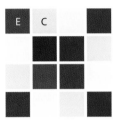

2. Sew the 2″ squares together, working across the block in 4 rows; press. Sew the rows together and press.

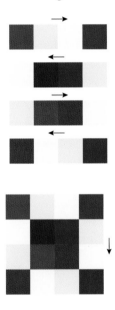

3. Repeat Steps 1 and 2 to make 49 Sixteen-Patch blocks. The blocks should measure 6½″ × 6½″, including the ¼″ seam allowance.

HALF SIXTEEN-PATCH BLOCKS

1. Lay out 4 assorted C's with 4 assorted E's to form half of a Sixteen-Patch block.

2. Sew the C and E squares together, working across the block in 2 rows; press. Sew the rows together and press. Repeat for a total of 7 half Sixteen-Patch blocks. The blocks should measure 3½″ × 6½″, including the ¼″ seam allowance.

QUILT ASSEMBLY

Refer to the quilt photo (page 44) and the quilt assembly diagram (below).

1. Lay out the quilt, alternating 7 half Sixteen-Patch blocks with 6 assorted A's for row 1. Alternate 7 Rail blocks with 6 Nine-Patch blocks in rows 2, 4, 6, 8, 10, 12, and 14. Alternate 7 Sixteen-Patch blocks with 6 Rail blocks in rows 3, 5, 7, 9, 11, 13, and 15.

2. Sew the blocks together in each row and press the seam allowances toward the Rail blocks. Sew the rows together and press the seams in one direction.

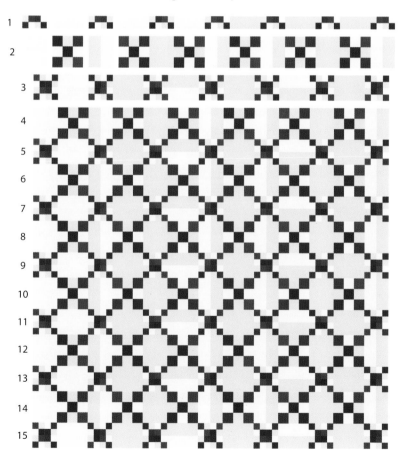

FINISHING UP

Refer to Finishing Up (pages 17–19) for details on completing your quilt.

1. Piece the backing fabric with 2 horizontal seams.

2. Layer the quilt top, batting, and backing fabric and baste.

3. Quilt as desired.

4. Bind using a ¼″ seam allowance.

5. Don't forget your quilt label.

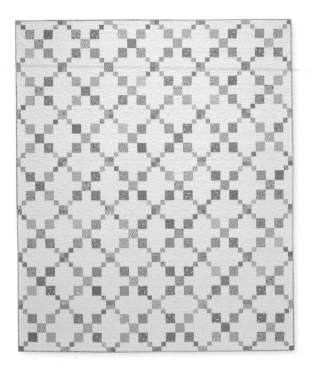

Made by Jean Welch and machine quilted by Nana's Quilt Shop

Jean used white background fabric to highlight the 1930s prints she loves (6½ yards are needed if using one light fabric).

Made by Meghan Welch and machine quilted by Donald Bunn

Alternating white chain blocks with blue, Meghan created a dynamic quilt.

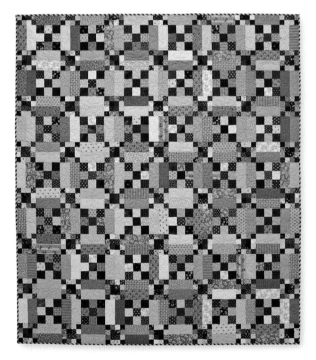

Made by Linda Davis and machine quilted by Margaret Landon

Linda chose to use two main colors of reproduction fabrics for her version of this quilt.

Made by Peggy Davis

For her quilt, Peggy chose to use a dark background with light chains crossing the quilt.

SIMPLE PLEASURES

Made by Nancy Murty and machine quilted by MaryKay Kaczmarek

▪ Simple Pleasures ▪

For many of us, quilting is counted among the simple pleasures we enjoy. There is something therapeutic about working with needle and thread that allows our mind to settle and escape our busy lives.

MATERIALS

Light tan: 1 yard for Star blocks and flying geese connectors

Medium tan: ⅔ yard for Star blocks

Dark tan: 1 yard for flying geese units and half-square triangle units

Rust: 1 yard for flying geese units and half-square triangle units

Gold print #1: ½ yard for four-patch units

Gold print #2: ½ yard for four-patch units

Dark purple: ⅝ yard for Star block points

Red purple: ½ yard for Star blocks

Brown print: ⅓ yard for Star block centers

Inner border: ⅝ yard

Outer border: 1⅓ yards

Binding: ⅞ yard

Backing: 4¾ yards

Batting: 74" × 84"

Quick Quarter II tool (*optional*)

CUTTING

The letter following each cut size corresponds to the letters in the block assembly diagrams.

Light tan
- Cut 3 strips 3¼" × width of fabric; subcut into:

  30 squares 3¼" × 3¼" (A)

  1 rectangle 4½" × 2½" (B)

  6 squares 2½" × 2½" (C)

- Cut 7 strips 2½" × width of fabric; subcut into:

  48 rectangles 4½" × 2½" (B)

  16 squares 2½" × 2½" (C)

Medium tan
- Cut 8 strips 2½" × width of fabric; subcut into:

  120 squares 2½" × 2½" (D)

Dark tan
- Cut 4 strips 5¼" × width of fabric; subcut into:

  25 squares 5¼" × 5¼" (E)

- Cut 2 strips 3¼" × width of fabric; subcut into:

  22 squares 3¼" × 3¼" (F)

Rust
- Cut 2 strips 3¼" × width of fabric; subcut into:

  22 squares 3¼" × 3¼" (G)

- Cut 8 strips 2⅞" × width of fabric; subcut into:

  100 squares 2⅞" × 2⅞" (H)

Gold print
From each fabric:

- Cut 4 strips 2½" × width of fabric; subcut into:

  60 squares 2½" × 2½" (I & J)

Dark purple
- Cut 5 strips 3¼" × width of fabric; subcut into:

  60 squares 3¼" × 3¼" (K)

Red purple
- Cut 3 strips 3¼" × width of fabric; subcut into:

  30 squares 3¼" × 3¼" (L)

Brown print
- Cut 2 strips 2½" × width of fabric; subcut into:

  30 squares 2½" × 2½" (M)

Inner border
- Cut 6 strips 2½" × width of fabric.

Outer border
- Cut 8 strips 6½" × width of fabric.

Binding
- Cut 8 strips 3" × width of fabric.

PIECED BLOCKS

Follow the arrows in each diagram for pressing direction.

STAR BLOCKS

1. Pair 30 K's with 30 A's and follow Steps 1 and 2 for half-square triangle units (pages 9 and 10) to make 60 dark purple / tan half-square triangle units; press.

2. Pair 30 K's with 30 L's to make 60 dark purple / red-purple half-square triangle units; press.

3. Using the Quick Quarter tool or a regular quilting ruler, mark the diagonal of the 60 dark purple / red-purple half-square triangle units (page 9, Step 1). Pair a marked dark purple / red-purple half-square triangle unit with a dark purple / light tan half-square triangle unit. The dark purple fabrics should *not* be face to face; instead, nest seams together. Sew on the outside drawn lines. Cut along the center dashed line to separate. Press the seams toward the darker half. Trim the dog-ears even with the square. Repeat to create 120 quarter-square triangle units that measure 2½″ × 2½″, including the ¼″ seam allowance.

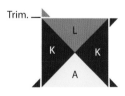

TIP

The Sewline Fabric Pencil (by Westek Corporation) with white or pink lead is great when marking dark fabrics.

4. Following the diagram for placement, lay out 4 quarter-square triangle units, 4 D's, and 1 M to create the Star block.

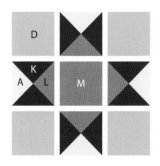

5. Working across in 3 rows, sew the units together and press. Sew the 3 rows together and press. Repeat to make 30 Star blocks that measure 6½″ × 6½″, including the ¼″ seam allowance.

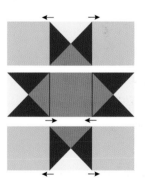

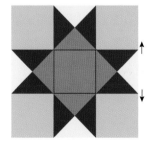

FLYING GEESE UNITS

1. Working with the 25 E's and 100 H's, make 98 flying geese units (page 10). (You will have 2 units left over.)

2. Sew a flying geese unit to each side of the 49 B's and press. Repeat to make 49 units that measure 4½" × 6½", including the ¼" seam allowance.

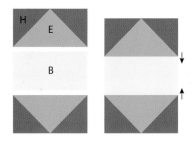

FOUR-PATCH UNITS

1. Set aside 2 I's and 2 J's for quilt assembly. With right sides together, pair each remaining I with a J. Sew together and press the seam allowances toward the darker fabric. Repeat, joining all remaining gold print squares to make 58 I/J units.

2. Set aside 18 I/J units for quilt assembly. Pair up and sew the 40 remaining I/J units to make 20 four-patch units, nesting the seams in the center; press.

HALF-SQUARE TRIANGLE UNITS

1. Make 44 half-square triangle units (pages 9 and 10) from 22 F's and 22 G's. Trim the half-square triangle units to 2½" × 2½".

2. Sew an F/G half-square triangle unit to each side of the 22 C's and press.

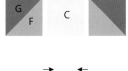

QUILT ASSEMBLY

Refer to the quilt photo (page 49) and the quilt assembly diagram (next page).

SEWING THE CENTER

Lay out the Star blocks, flying geese units, four-patch units, half-square triangle units, and the units and squares that were set aside. Sew the units in each horizontal row and press the seam allowances toward the flying geese units. Sew the rows together and press the seams in one direction.

BORDERS

1. Join the 6 inner border strips to create one long continuous strip, using diagonal seams (page 16). Cut 2 strips 2½" × 60½" for the sides and 2 strips 2½" × 54½" for the top and bottom.

2. Sew the 60½" inner border strips to the sides of the pieced quilt center and press the seam allowances toward the inner border. Sew the 54½" inner border strips to the top and bottom and press the seams toward the inner border.

3. Join the 8 outer border strips to create one long continuous strip, using diagonal seams (page 16). Cut 2 strips 6½" × 64½" for the sides and 2 strips 6½" × 66½" for the top and bottom. Sew the outer border strips to the sides of the quilt and press the seams toward the outer border. Sew the outer border strips to the top and bottom of the quilt and press toward the outer border.

FINISHING UP

Refer to Finishing Up (pages 17–19) for details on completing your quilt.

1. Piece the backing fabric with one vertical seam.

2. Layer the quilt top, batting, and backing fabric and baste.

3. Quilt as desired.

4. Bind using a ½″ seam allowance.

5. Don't forget your quilt label.

Made by Peggy Davis

Peggy made her version of this quilt using scraps from her collection.

Made by Jean Welch and Linda Davis, and machine quilted by Margaret Landon

Jean and Linda selected their fabrics to highlight the larger star in their quilt.

PERENNIAL TIES

Made by Nancy Murty

Finished block: 12″ × 12″

Finished quilt: 38″ × 38″

Skill level: Intermediate

Our quilting sisterhood has blessed us with cherished connections. We've shared many good times and know we can depend
on one another. Like the perennials in our gardens, these sisters
are not always visible—sometimes they're miles away, or months
pass between visits. We know, however, that as sure as the tulips
will bloom in the garden, our quilting sisters will be there for us.

MATERIALS

Cream: ½ yard for block background and narrow sashing

Tan: ½ yard for block background
basket

Brown: ½ yard for basket and
border corners

Brown floral: ⅝ yard for outer
border

Pumpkin: ⅛ yard for basket

Red: ½ yard for flowers, center
squares, and inner border

Gold: ⅛ yard for flower centers

Green: ⅓ yard or scraps for leaves

Yellow-green print: 1 fat quarter
for stems

Binding: ½ yard

Backing: 1¼ yards

Batting: 42″ × 42″

CUTTING

*The letter following each cut size cor-
responds to the letters in the block
assembly diagrams.*

Cream
- Cut 1 strip 8½″ × width of fabric;
  subcut into:

  8 rectangles 4½″ × 8½″ (A)

- Cut 2 strips 2½″ × width of fabric;
  subcut into:

  4 rectangles 12½″ × 2½″ (B)

Tan
- Cut 1 strip 6⅞″ × width of fabric;
  subcut into:

  2 squares 6⅞″ × 6⅞″; cut in half
  diagonally (C)

  4 squares 3¼″ × 3¼″ (D)

- Cut 1 strip 4½″ × width of fabric;
  subcut into:

  4 squares 4½″ × 4½″ (E)

  8 rectangles 2½″ × 4½″ (F)

Brown
- Cut 1 strip 6½″ × width of fabric;
  subcut into:

  4 squares 6½″ × 6½″ (G)

  4 squares 3¼″ × 3¼″ (H)

- Cut 1 strip 2½″ × width of fabric;
  subcut into:

  8 rectangles 4⅞″ × 2½″ (I)

Brown floral
- Cut 4 strips 4½″ × width of fabric;
  subcut into:

  4 strips 4½″ × 26½″ (J) outer border

Pumpkin
- Cut 2 squares 2⅞″ × 2⅞″; cut in
  half diagonally (K).

- Cut 4 squares 2½″ × 2½″ (L).

Red
- Cut 4 strips 2½″ × width of fabric;
  subcut into:

  4 strips 2½″ × 26½″ (M) inner
  border

  5 squares 2½″ × 2½″ (N)

Binding
- Cut 4 strips 3″ × width of fabric.

BASKET BLOCKS

Follow the arrows in each diagram for pressing direction.

1. The I pieces need to be specially cut before the Basket block construction can begin. With right sides together, pair the rectangles into 4 sets of 2 rectangles each. Position the ruler at a 45° angle by lining up the ruler's 45° line with the edge of the rectangle and in the corner of the fabric rectangle. Using a rotary cutter, remove the corner triangle. Repeat for all 4 sets of rectangles to make 2 mirror-image pieces for each block.

2. Select 4 D's and 4 H's. Construct 8 half-square triangle units (pages 9 and 10) and press. Trim each unit to 2½″ × 2½″.

3. Lay out the various components to create the Basket block.

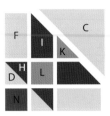

4. Set C to the side. Sew the components together, working across in 3 rows; press. Sew the 3 rows together, nesting the seams between the rows; press. Sew C to the basket unit to complete the block. Press the seam toward the large triangle. Repeat for a total of 4 Basket blocks, each measuring 8½″ × 8½″, including the ¼″ seam allowance.

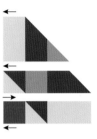

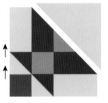

5. Lay out the 2 A pieces and 1 E piece with the Basket block. Sew together, working across in 2 rows; press. Sew the 2 rows together and press. Repeat for the remaining 3 Basket blocks. The blocks should measure 12½″ × 12½″, including seam allowances.

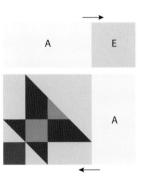

ADD THE APPLIQUÉ

Prepare the appliqués, using the appliqué method of your choice (pages 11–15).

1. Prepare 16 bias stems, each ¼″ × 5″ (page 11). Using the method of your choice, trace and prepare the appliqués (page 58).

2. Follow the quilt photo for placing the appliqués on the pieced Basket blocks. Position the stems first, followed by the other appliqués. Repeat to make 4 appliquéd blocks.

FINISHING THE QUILT CENTER

1. Lay out the appliqué blocks, 4 B pieces, and the remaining N.

2. Sew together into 3 rows and press.

3. Sew together the 3 rows and press. The quilt center should measure 26½″ × 26½″.

BORDERS

1. Sew 4 M's to 4 J's to create 4 border units. Press the seams toward J.

2. Lay out the G pieces and the 4 J/M border units around the pieced quilt center. Sew the components together, working across in 3 rows. Press the seams toward the pieced border units.

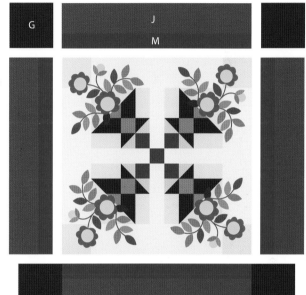

3. Sew the 3 rows together and press the seams toward the border. The quilt top should measure 38½″ × 38½″, including the ¼″ seam allowance.

FINISHING UP

Refer to Finishing Up (pages 17–19) for details on completing your quilt.

1. Layer the quilt top, batting, and backing fabric and baste.

2. Quilt as desired.

3. Bind using a ½″ seam allowance.

4. Don't forget your quilt label.

Made by Linda Davis and machine quilted by Judy Schryver

Linda added beads to the center of her flowers for a little sparkle.

Made by Jean Welch

Although Jean's flowers are almost identical to Linda's, isn't it fun to see how different fabric choices change the overall look?

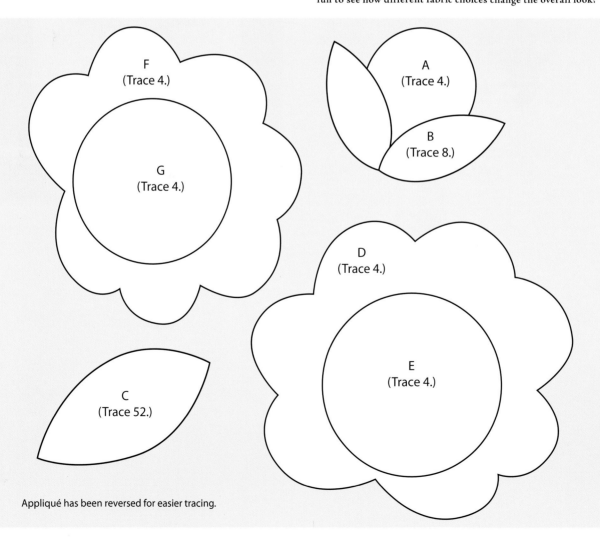

F
(Trace 4.)

G
(Trace 4.)

A
(Trace 4.)

B
(Trace 8.)

D
(Trace 4.)

E
(Trace 4.)

C
(Trace 52.)

Appliqué has been reversed for easier tracing.

PULLING WEEDS

Made by Linda Davis and machine quilted by Lynn Artieri

· Pulling Weeds ·

Finished block: 12" × 12"

Finished quilt: 67" × 67"

Skill level: Intermediate

If you're like me, childhood memories are full of time spent doing chores with family. I recall, quite vividly, pulling weeds in the garden, feeding the chickens, collecting the eggs, helping with the laundry, and the list goes on. I didn't realize it at the time, but during all of these chores, we were talking, sharing, and even laughing. Indeed, they are some of the fondest memories I have.

As you choose your fabrics, put all of them together on your sewing table or even in a pile on the floor. Then pull the fabrics that don't fit with the others—these are your "weeds." Just like the garden, your quilt will be that much better from the little bit of time you spend "weeding" your fabrics.

MATERIALS

Pale green: 1½ yards for border

Light green: 1⅓ yards for blocks and border corners

Greens: ¾ yard each of 4 for blocks

Reds: ½ yard each of 4 for blocks and flowers

Turquoise blue: ¼ yard for flower hearts

Green: ½ yard for main bias stem

Dark green: ¼ yard for flower bias stems

Binding: ¾ yard

Backing: 4¼ yards

Batting: 75" × 75"

CUTTING

The letter following each cut size corresponds to the letters in the block assembly diagrams.

Pale green
- Cut 4 strips 10" × *length of fabric*; subcut into:

  4 strips 10" × 48½" (A) for the border

Light green
- Cut 1 strip 10" × width of fabric; subcut into:

  4 squares 10" × 10" (B)
- Cut 5 strips 5¼" × width of fabric; subcut into:

  32 squares 5¼" × 5¼" (C)

Green
From each of the 4 fabrics:

- Cut 2 strips 5¼" × width of fabric; subcut into:

  8 squares 5¼" × 5¼" (D) and 8 squares 2½" × 2½"
- Cut 2 strips 2½" × width of fabric; subcut into:

  32 squares 2½" × 2½" (E)

Red
From each of the 4 fabrics:

- Cut 3 strips 2½" × width of fabric; subcut into:

  40 squares 2½" × 2½" (F)

Binding
- Cut 7 strips 3" × width of fabric.

PIECED BLOCKS

Follow the arrows in each diagram for pressing direction.

1. Select 10 matching E's and 10 matching F's. With right sides together, join the green and red squares and press. Repeat to create 10 two-patch units.

2. Pair up 2 two-patch units with the green squares opposite the red squares; sew together and press. You should have 5 green/red four-patch units. Repeat to make 16 sets, each containing 5 matching green/red four-patch units.

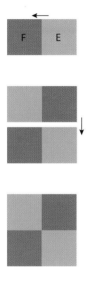

3. Select 2 matching D's and 2 matching C's. Construct 4 half-square triangle units (pages 9 and 10) and trim to 4½″ × 4½″. Repeat to create 16 sets, each containing 4 matching half-square triangle units.

4. Lay out 1 set of 5 matching green/red four-patch units and 1 set of 4 matching half-square triangle units to create the Jacob's Ladder block.

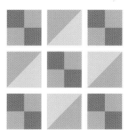

5. Working across in 3 rows, sew the units together and press. Sew the 3 rows together and press. Repeat for a total of 16 pieced blocks. Blocks should measure 12½″ × 12½″, including the ¼″ seam allowance.

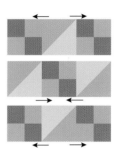

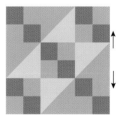

QUILT CENTER ASSEMBLY

Refer to the quilt photo (page 59) and the quilt assembly diagram (next page).

1. Lay out the 16 pieced blocks in 4 rows, rotating them as shown.

2. Sew the blocks together into rows and press the seam allowances in opposite directions for each row. Sew 4 rows together and press the seams in one direction. The pieced quilt center should measure 48½" × 48½".

APPLIQUÉD BORDER

Prepare the appliqués, using the appliqué method of your choice (pages 11–15).

1. For the appliqués (pattern pullout page P2), cut along the center dashed line of the border patterns to separate. Tape the 2 sections together as directed on the pullout.

2. Prepare 4 bias stems ½" × at least 66" long and 28 bias stems ¼" × at least 7½" long (page 11). Mark the center of the 4 long bias stems with a pin.

3. Sew a B to each end of 2 A pieces and press the seam allowances toward the square, B. These will become the top and bottom borders and should measure 10" × 67½".

4. Fold a pieced 67½" border section in half and lightly press to mark the center. Fold in half along the length and lightly press to mark the center. Repeat for the second pieced border section.

5. Fold the 2 remaining A rectangles in half, marking the center in both directions.

6. Position a 67½" border section over the border pattern, lining up the centers. Using the pattern as a guide, position the main stem first, followed by the smaller stems. Use Roxanne Glue Baste-It to hold the stems in place.

7. Pin the flower units and leaves in place along the main stem. Do not place the heart in the corner; it will be added in a later step.

8. Flip the pattern page over; repeat Steps 6 and 7 for the second half of the border.

9. Stitch the appliqués in place.

10. Repeat Steps 6–9 for the second 67½" border section.

11. Repeat Steps 6–9 for the side borders A, this time positioning only 5 flower units on each border. Do not work beyond the last 2" on each end of the 2 shorter borders. The corner appliqués will be added after the border sections have been sewn to the quilt center.

Sewing the Borders to the Quilt Center

1. With a safety pin, securely fasten the main vine away from each end of the 48½″ borders. This will prevent the main stem from being caught in the seams.

2. Sew a 48½″ appliquéd border unit to the sides of the quilt center and press the seam allowances toward the border.

3. Sew a 67½″ border to the top and bottom of the quilt center and press the seams toward the border.

4. Finish by appliquéing the remaining flower units, leaves, and hearts to each corner of the border.

Finishing Up

Refer to Finishing Up (pages 17–19) for details on completing your quilt.

1. Piece the backing fabric with one vertical seam.

2. Layer the quilt top, batting, and backing fabric and baste.

3. Quilt as desired.

4. Bind using a ½″ seam allowance.

5. Don't forget your quilt label.

Pin end of vine away from seam allowance.

Pin end of vine away from seam allowance.

Dinner for Two

Made by Nancy Murty

■ Dinner for Two ■

Finished blocks: 12″ × 12″

Finished table runner: 17″ × 51″

Skill level: Intermediate

In my family, dinnertime has always been much more than just a meal. It's a time to share the day's triumphs and challenges, time to share a laugh or tell an old story. I love the idea of incorporating quilts into everyday life, and what better way than with a table runner. Pick fabrics that complement your decor, or make several in different colors to highlight the seasons. Have dinner for two tonight but order out—you've been sewing all day.

MATERIALS

Cream: ½ yard for block background

Pale pink: ⅓ yard for setting triangles

Pink: ⅜ yard for setting triangles

Red: ¼ yard for blocks

Green: ¼ yard for blocks

Brown: ½ yard for blocks

Binding: ⅓ yard

Backing: 1⅔ yards

Batting: 25″ × 59″

CUTTING

The letter following each cut size corresponds to the letters in the block assembly diagrams.

Cream
■ Cut 1 strip 4½″ × width of fabric; subcut into:

12 rectangles 2½″ × 4½″ (A)

■ Cut 2 strips 2⅞″ × width of fabric; subcut into:

12 squares 2⅞″ × 2⅞″ (B)

12 squares 2⅞″ × 2⅞″; cut in half diagonally (C)

Pale pink
■ Cut 2 squares 9¾″ × 9¾″; cut in half diagonally in both directions (D).

Pink
■ Cut 4 squares 6½″ × 6½″ (E).

Red
■ Cut 12 squares 2½″ × 2½″ (F).

Green
■ Cut 3 squares 5¼″ × 5¼″ (G).

Brown
■ Cut 1 strip 4⅞″ × width of fabric; subcut into:

6 squares 4⅞″ × 4⅞″; cut in half diagonally (H)

■ Cut 3 squares 4½″ × 4½″ (I).

Binding
■ Cut 4 strips 2″ × width of fabric.

PIECED BLOCKS

Follow the arrows in each diagram for pressing direction.

1. Follow the Flying Geese method (page 10), using 12 B's and 3 G's to construct 12 flying geese units.

2. Sew an A to each flying geese unit and press. Each geese/A unit should measure 4½″ × 4½″.

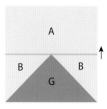

3. Lay out 1 F with 2 C's and 1 H.

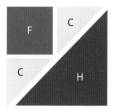

4. With right sides together, sew a C to the right side of F and press. Sew the second C to the bottom of F and press.

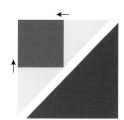

5. Sew H to the triangle unit and press.

6. Repeat Steps 1–5 to make 12 corner units. The units should measure 4½″ × 4½″.

7. Following the block diagram, lay out 4 flying geese units, 4 corner units, and an I piece.

8. Working across in 3 rows, sew the units together and press. Join the 3 rows and press.

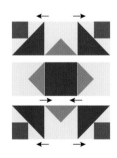

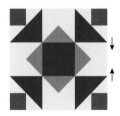

9. Repeat Steps 1–8 to construct 3 blocks that measure 12½″ × 12½″, including seam allowances.

FINAL ASSEMBLY

Follow the arrows in each diagram for pressing direction.

1. To create the pieced setting triangles, lay out 2 D's and 1 E. Sew a D to the E, matching the square corner of the triangle with a corner of the square; press. Sew a second D to the unit and press. Repeat to make 4 pieced setting-triangle units.

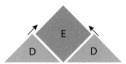

2. Lay out the 4 pieced setting triangles and 3 pieced blocks. Working in 3 diagonal rows, sew the setting triangles to the blocks and press. Sew the 3 rows together, nesting the seams; press.

FINISHING UP

Refer to Finishing Up (pages 17–19) for details on completing your table runner.

1. Layer the table runner, batting, and backing fabric and baste.

2. Quilt as desired.

3. Bind using a ¼″ seam allowance.

4. Don't forget your quilt label.

FORGET ME KNOT

Made by Nancy Murty

Finished block: 18″ × 18″

Finished quilt: 72″ × 72″

Skill level: Intermediate

My grandmother's first quilts were made for her hope chest, with the knowledge in her heart that she would someday meet my grandfather and start a family. I made a special quilt for my husband, Paul, when we were dating, and we received a masterpiece from my mother when we were married. All of these are beautiful, cherished quilts that celebrate another special bond, the bond between husband and wife.

Forget Me Knot is in honor of the timeless quilting tradition of making quilts to celebrate marriages and the beginning of families. This quilt is a little more involved than some of the other projects in the book, but I think it's worth it. It will certainly be cherished for generations to come.

MATERIALS

Cream: 2½ yards for appliqué background and flying geese

Beige: 2¾ yards for appliqué background and flying geese background

Tan: 1 yard for narrow borders

Orange: ⅛ yard each of 4 fabrics for small flowers

Gold: ⅓ yard for small flower centers

Dark purple: ⅝ yard for wig rose

Red purple: ⅞ yard for outer part of large flower center and binding

Wine: ¼ yard for large flower center

Yellow green: ½ yard for leaves

Green #1: ½ yard for leaves

Green #2: ⅓ yard for stems

Backing: 4½ yards

Batting: 80″ × 80″

CUTTING

Cream

- Cut 5 strips 10¼″ × width of fabric; subcut into:

  18 squares 10¼″ × 10¼″ (A)

- Cut 4 strips 7¼″ × width of fabric; subcut into:

  18 squares 7¼″ × 7¼″ (B)

Beige

- Cut 5 strips 10¼″ × width of fabric; subcut into:

  18 squares 10¼″ × 10¼″ (C)

- Cut 1 strip 6½″ × width of fabric; subcut into:

  4 squares 6½″ × 6½″ (D)

  8 rectangles 6½″ × 2″ (E) (may need to cut 1 rectangle from leftover fabric)

- Cut 8 strips 3⅞″ × width of fabric; subcut into:

  72 squares 3⅞″ × 3⅞″ (F)

Tan

- Cut 14 strips 2″ × width of fabric for narrow borders.

Red purple

- Cut 8 strips 2″ × width of fabric for binding.

APPLIQUÉ BLOCKS

Prepare the appliqués, using the appliqué method of your choice (pages 11–15).

1. Construct 36 half-square triangle units (pages 9 and 10) from the 18 A pieces and the 18 C pieces; press. Trim the units to 9½″ × 9½″.

2. Arrange as shown. Sew 4 half-square triangle units together to create a large square; press. Repeat to make 9 large squares that measure 18½″ × 18½″.

3. Prepare 72 bias stems, each ¼″ × 6″ (page 11). Using the method of your choice, trace and prepare the appliqués (page 70).

4. Follow the quilt photo (page 67) and the quilt assembly diagram (page 70) for placing the appliqués on the large pieced square. Remember to position the stems first, followed by the other appliqués. Stitch the appliqués in place. Repeat to make 9 appliqué blocks.

QUILT ASSEMBLY

Sew together the appliqué blocks in 3 horizontal rows of 3 blocks each and press the seams in opposite directions, so they will nest together. Sew the 3 rows together and press the seams in one direction. The pieced quilt center should measure 54½″ × 54½″.

BORDERS

Follow the arrows in each diagram for pressing direction.

Inner Border

1. Join 6 of the narrow border strips, using diagonal seams (page 16). Cut into 2 strips 2″ × 54½″ for the sides and 2 strips 2″ × 57½″ for the top and bottom.

2. Sew 54½″ strips to the sides of the quilt center and press the seams toward the inner border.

3. Sew the 57½″ strips to the top and bottom of the quilt center and press the seams toward the inner border fabric. The quilt center should now measure 57½″ × 57½″.

Flying Geese Border

1. Follow the Flying Geese method (page 10), using 18 B's and 72 F's to construct 72 flying geese units that measure 3½″ × 6½″.

2. Lay out 18 flying geese units so that 2 sets of 9 geese point out from the center. Sew the geese together to create a strip; press. Sew an E piece to each end of the strip and press the seams toward the rectangles. Repeat to create a total of 4 flying geese border units.

3. Join a flying geese strip to each side of the quilt. Press the seams toward the inner border.

4. Sew a D to both ends of the 2 remaining flying geese strips and press the seams toward the square. Sew these strips to the top and bottom of the quilt and press the seams toward the quilt.

Outer Border

1. Join 8 of the narrow border strips, using diagonal seams (page 16). Cut this into 2 strips 2″ × 69½″ for the sides and 2 strips 2″ × 72½″ for the top and bottom of the quilt.

2. Sew the 69½″ strips to the sides of the quilt center and press the seams toward the outer border.

3. Sew the 72½" strips to the top and bottom of the quilt center and press the seams toward the outer border. The quilt should now measure 72½" × 72½".

FINISHING UP

Refer to Finishing Up (pages 17–19) for details on completing your quilt.

1. Piece the backing fabric with one vertical seam.

2. Layer the quilt top, batting, and backing fabric and baste.

3. Quilt as desired.

4. Bind using a ¼" seam allowance.

5. Don't forget your quilt label.

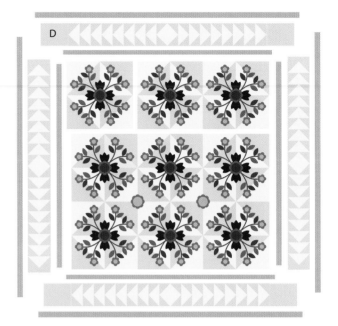

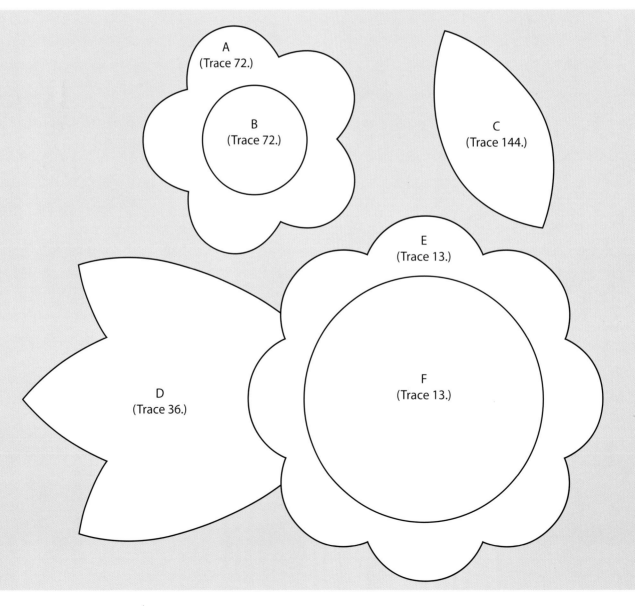

A
(Trace 72.)

B
(Trace 72.)

C
(Trace 144.)

E
(Trace 13.)

D
(Trace 36.)

F
(Trace 13.)

ABOUT THE AUTHOR

Born and raised in a rural section of New York state, Nancy Murty learned to sew at a very young age, making her first quilt as a young teenager. With the encouragement of her sister and mother, quilting quickly became a passion, as well as a family tradition.

Nancy began her professional quilting career in the summer of 1999 with the creation of Bee Creative Studio, which specializes in pictorial appliqué quilt patterns. Asked to design for Andover Fabrics in 2001, Nancy has enjoyed extending her artistic talents to create fun, whimsical collections to share with fellow quilters. In 2004, Nancy began to enter her quilts in national shows, earning many awards, including the Fairfield award for Contemporary Artistry at the International Quilt Festival in Houston.

Located in rural Farmington, New York, with her husband, Paul, Nancy greatly enjoys her time in the studio, which has a view overlooking the countryside and its seemingly endless inspiration. When not quilting, Nancy likes to spend her time painting, gardening, and visiting with family and friends.

Left: *My aunt, Jean Welch, and her sisters.*
Right: *Me and my sister, Peggy MacEwen.*

Great Titles *from* C&T PUBLISHING

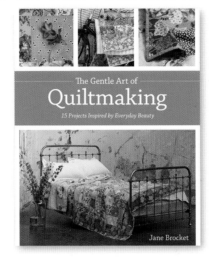

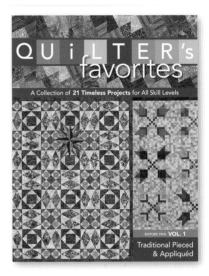

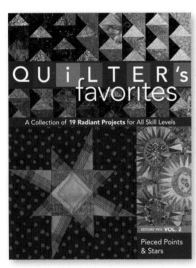

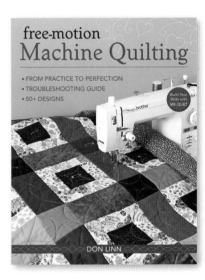

Available at your local retailer or **www.ctpub.com** *or* **800-284-1114**

For a list of other fine books from C&T Publishing, visit our website to view our catalog online.

C&T PUBLISHING, INC.

P.O. Box 1456
Lafayette, CA 94549
800-284-1114

Email: ctinfo@ctpub.com
Website: www.ctpub.com

C&T Publishing's professional photography services are now available to the public. Visit us at www.ctmediaservices.com.

Tips and Techniques can be found at www.ctpub.com > Consumer Resources > Quiltmaking Basics: Tips & Techniques for Quiltmaking & More

For quilting supplies:

COTTON PATCH

1025 Brown Ave.
Lafayette, CA 94549
Store: 925-284-1177
Mail order: 925-283-7883

Email: CottonPa@aol.com
Website: www.quiltusa.com

Note: Fabrics used in the quilts shown may not be currently available, as fabric manufacturers keep most fabrics in print for only a short time.